Native Americans

A Thematic Unit on Converging Cultures

Wendy S. Wilson and Lloyd M. Thompson

J. WESTON
WALCH
PUBLISHER

Portland, Maine

User's Guide
to
Walch Reproducible Books

As part of our general effort to provide educational materials which are as practical and economical as possible, we have designated this publication a "reproducible book." The designation means that purchase of the book includes purchase of the right to limited reproduction of all pages on which this symbol appears:

Here is the basic Walch policy: We grant to individual purchasers of this book the right to make sufficient copies of reproducible pages for use by all students of a single teacher. This permission is limited to a single teacher, and does not apply to entire schools or school systems, so institutions purchasing the book should pass the permission on to a single teacher. Copying of the book or its parts for resale is prohibited.

Any questions regarding this policy or requests to purchase further reproduction rights should be addressed to:

Permissions Editor
J. Weston Walch, Publisher
321 Valley Street • P. O. Box 658
Portland, Maine 04104-0658

1   2   3   4   5   6   7   8   9   10
ISBN 0-8251-3332-7
Copyright © 1997
J. Weston Walch, Publisher
P. O. Box 658 • Portland, Maine 04104-0658
Printed in the United States of America

Contents

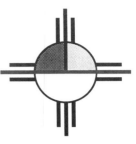

Credits

Dover Pictorial Archive: pages *viii*, 1, 7, 9, 11, 13, 15, 19, 21, 23, 24, 33, 45, 54, 55, 57, 58, 63, 68, 69, 73, 75, 85, 87, 95

Ohio Historical Society: page 3

Cahokia Mounds State Historic Site: page 4

Corel CD: pages 12, 27

Gilcrease Museum, Tulsa, OK: page 39

Library of Congress: pages 47, 49, 91, 100

Woolaroc Museum, Bartlesville, OK: page 66

Smithsonian Institution: page 77

To the Teacher

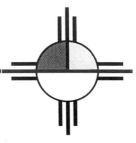

An important trend in education has been the recent emphasis on multiculturalism, particularly as it pertains to United States history.

As educators, we are sensitive to the diversity and richness of the variety of cultures that make up our nation. One common misconception, though, is that this diversity is a fairly recent phenomenon, impacting us only within the last two decades—or at most since the turn of the twentieth century with the peak years of immigration to this country. In reality, long before our "first" European immigrants arrived in 1492, there was an astounding diversity of culture among the people known as Native Americans.

Native Americans, or American Indians as some tribes prefer to be called, were comprised of groups that varied greatly in culture, lifestyle, and language. It has been estimated that there were as many as 500 tribal groups, with each as unique in its dress, appearance, and culture as people from the different European nations were.

Another common misconception is that these Native American cultures were static and unchanging. There was, however, movement, adaptation, and change among these cultures long before the arrival of Europeans.

American Indian tribes developed new crops, moved their people to new locations, built what could be called cities, and abandoned those cities just as we would find in a history of early civilizations in the Middle East, Europe, Asia, or Africa. The history of America did not suddenly begin with the European contact, but rather it had existed for many thousands of years before the fifteenth and sixteenth centuries. The European contact added new experiences, new changes, new challenges, and often new tragedies to the already long history of the Native Americans.

The purpose of this reproducible book is to examine the culture of Native American groups at the point of their contact with a European culture. The approach used is that of case study, since not every single group can be studied due to the variety and number. European exploration and motivation will also be discussed. In short, this will be a study of cultures in convergence, American Indian and European.

This book can be used to study exploration, Native American culture and history, United States geography, and United States history. Each unit contains a teacher's guide with background information, a reproducible student information sheet, and a series of reproducible activities based upon that unit. The activities are presented at different skill levels and are also designed to encompass multiple intelligences and talents to allow teachers to individualize classroom instruction.

Very often, the story of Native Americans and their treatment by European newcomers and the United States government itself is a story of cultural destruction and betrayal. Feelings of anger can and do still exist.

Our focus is not to dwell on the iniquities of the past, but to demonstrate a common richness of culture that goes far back into the history of human habitation on the North American continent, before the European explorers, before the formation of the nation of the United States. The diversity of the Native American tribes and their contribution to the culture of our nation is part of all our peoples' heritage. With the recognition of this contribution can come understanding and appreciation of all the groups which make up our nation's rich past and future promise.

vii

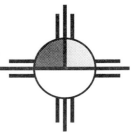

To the Student _____

Many thousands of years ago, hunters crossed over from Siberia into what is now called North America. They came across the **Bering Strait land bridge**, created during the last Ice Age. These prehistoric people wore animal skins and carried stone weapons and tools. They traveled in search of large animals, such as the woolly mammoth. They needed the flesh, bones, and hides for food, clothing, and shelter. These nomads were the first Americans, the ancestors of people now known as **Native Americans,** or **American Indians**.

On the Move

The ancient world was a time of **migration**. Humans spread from Africa, where the species originated, in search of new food sources and new lands. Even when a group settled in a place and developed a **civilization**, migrations and movements continued. In short, the world has always been a place of flux and change. People migrated, invaded, traded, and communicated with one another. Archaeology and other sciences show that there was a constant interchange among ancient peoples.

Native Americans have always been a people in movement—sometimes willingly and sometimes due to force. From the beginning, they have shown a remarkable adaptation to their environment. Their respect for nature and careful use of resources can provide valuable lessons for us today.

Rich in Diversity

The history of the world is not only a story of people in movement. It is also a story of

human **diversity**, with many unique **cultures** and lifestyles. Egypt had the Pyramid Age. The Chinese civilization perfected casting in bronze and weaving silk. The Native Americans were a people of great diversity. At one time, as many as 500 different **tribes**, with 300 languages, covered North America. The tribes were as different as the Babylonians were from the builders of Stonehenge. The stereotype of a Native American with feathers and a tomahawk grew out of Buffalo Bill's Wild West Show (popular around the turn of the twentieth century) and Hollywood movies.

The richness and diversity of Native American culture helped shape our national heritage. As groups arrived in the Americas—mainly from Europe—their culture came into contact with the Native American way of life. Often the result was conflict, destruction, and **displacement** of the native peoples. But cultures in contact also led to interchange. Native ways of life were altered by technology, by new kinds of plants and animals, and by new **ideologies**. In turn, the explorers were changed by the native peoples' foods, knowledge of nature, and capacity for survival.

Now we will explore these early cultures in convergence. We will use case studies of Native American groups at the point of contact with European explorers and settlers. We will examine the lifestyle of tribal groups before European contact. We will look at the European motivations for

(continued)

© 1997 J. Weston Walch, Publisher   *Native Americans:*
A Thematic Unit on Converging Cultures

Name _____   Date _____

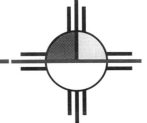

To the Student _____
(continued)

Culture Areas of Native Americans

© 1997 J. Weston Walch, Publisher

(continued)

*Native Americans:
A Thematic Unit on Converging Cultures*

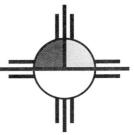

To the Student _____
(continued)

exploring and settling a specific area. And we will examine the lasting cultural results of the contact between the newcomers and the original inhabitants. We hope this study will reinforce the concept that American history reaches far back in time. Our history reaches back to those first migrants from Asia who crossed the Bering Strait land bridge thousands of years before Europeans first set foot in North and South America. They set the original pattern, since repeated in wave upon wave of people who have come seeking a better life.

Glossary of Terms

Bering Strait land bridge: Land area connecting Asia and North America during the last Ice Age.

civilization: A population that has attained a relatively high level of cultural and technological development, usually marked by a written language.

culture: A particular form or level of a civilization, such as a hunting and food-gathering culture.

displacement: Removal.

diversity: The state of being different.

ideology: A manner of thinking characteristic of a group or culture.

migration: Movement from one place to another.

Native American/American Indian: Two terms used to describe the original inhabitants of the Americas. *Native American* is deemed more politically correct, since *Indian* was a term used by Columbus when he thought he had reached Asia. Some tribes prefer *American Indian*. Many scientists refer to Native American people as *Amerinds* or *Amerindians*.

tribe: A social group made up of several families, clans, or generations.

1. Adena–Hopewell–Mississippian Cultures

Pottery from the early Mississippian culture

Adena–Hopewell–Mississippian Cultures: Exploding the Myth of Primitiveness

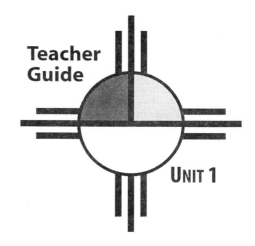

Teacher Guide

Unit 1

The objective of this introductory unit is to give students a sense of Native American culture before the arrival of Europeans. Although the pre-Columbian cultures of Central and South America have been emphasized in the secondary curriculum, North America has been neglected. This is probably because the diversity of Native American cultures in North America makes study difficult and also because, unlike the Maya or Aztec civilizations, North American cultures left no large, highly visible artifacts and structures.

The Student Information Sheet introduces students to an Indian culture that did produce highly visible records of its existence. The Adena, Hopewell, and Mississippian cultures, known collectively as the Mound Builders, flourished from approximately 500 B.C.E. to 1700 C.E. They engaged in many of the activities that scholars attribute to a "civilization"—large-scale trade, political organization, and religious practices that included ritual burial of the dead. As far as historians know, however, the Mound Builders did not have a written language.

Preparation for This Unit

We highly recommend that you lead your students in discussing what defines a civilization. The Europeans who first came to North America wrote that American Indians were barbaric and uncivilized and, in fact, incapable of becoming civilized. Upon what standards were Europeans basing this judgment?

Student Activities

Worksheet 1 centers on what constitutes a civilization—what qualifies it as a valid type of study in social studies curriculum. Students are asked to compare Cahokia with Ancient Egypt, a common topic for study in history courses. Worksheet 2 examines a thorny ethical issue: Is it justifiable to excavate Indian burial sites for scientific study? Many Native American groups feel that this is an unjustifiable desecration of the graves of their ancestors. A good preparation for this exercise would be to have students read the first chapter of *Talking God* by Tony Hillerman (Harper and Row, 1989). The roles in the simulated court case in Worksheet 2 can be expanded or contracted to fit your own classroom situation. You might even invite another class to act as a impartial jury.

Adena–Hopewell–Mississippian Cultures:
Exploding the Myth of Primitiveness

Aerial photo of the Great Serpent Mound, southern Ohio

Study of the **pre-Columbian** civilizations of the Maya, Aztec, and Inca is common. The advanced culture of these civilizations makes them exceptional among Amerindian cultures. They can be compared to civilizations in Europe, Asia, and Africa. North American Indians may not have attained the same level of urban development as these Central and South American cultures—with two notable exceptions: the Anasazi of the Southwest and the Mound Builders of the Midwest and Southeast.

These people, who are known as the Mound Builders, actually comprise three successive Indian cultures: the Adena (500 B.C.E.–1 C.E.), the Hopewell (100 B.C.E.–500 C.E.), and the Mississippian (1000–1700 C.E.). All three cultures were alike in that they lived along rivers of central North America. All three lived in village communities. All had an economy based on farming, foraging, and trade. And all constructed earthen mounds as places of worship and burial.

The Environment

The Mississippi River and its tributaries, including the Ohio and the Tennessee Rivers, provided the Mound Builders with fertile lands for agriculture and waterways for trade. The Hopewell peoples traded extensively from as far west as the Rocky Mountains, east to the Atlantic Ocean, and south to the Gulf of Mexico. They brought **obsidian** from the Yellowstone area for blades and spearheads. They brought copper from the Great Lakes, used for ornaments and ceremonial objects. And they brought seashells from the Atlantic Ocean and the Gulf of Mexico.

The Adena and Hopewell did not build large communities. They lived in small villages with probably no more than 400 inhabitants. They constructed earthworks that were used for burials and, probably, religious ceremonies. The Hopewell were particularly impressive surveyors. The constructed hundreds of mounds with a precision that, according to one modern

(continued)

Adena–Hopewell–Mississippian Cultures:
Exploding the Myth of Primitiveness *(continued)*

Cahokia

engineer, required a good knowledge of geometry.*

The Mississippian culture followed these master builders with even more extraordinary structures. They built flat-topped, pyramidal structures. Thus, historians refer to them as the Temple Mound Builders. The greatest of all of these pyramids was located at Cahokia, in what is today Illinois.

Mississippian Culture at Its Height

Cahokia was near the convergence of the Missouri, Illinois, and Mississippi rivers. It was the largest urban center in North America before 1800. Inhabited for over 700 years, it was the center of the Mississippian culture from approximately 850 to 1150 C.E. Population esti-

mates vary. Probably more than 10,000 people lived there, with perhaps 10,000 more living in the surrounding villages.

This population was sustained by a new strain of corn that grew in only 120 days. The Mississippians also grew beans. The beans and the corn provided all the protein necessary for survival. The people of Cahokia not only farmed extensively, they also fished and hunted, traded, and practiced crafts. They worked to sustain an elite population of chiefs and religious leaders.

These leaders may have lived in a special area of the city surrounded by a wooden stockade. At the head of the Mississippian social system was an absolute ruler. The ruler lived in a 105-foot-long wooden building on top of

---

* The engineer was James A. Marshall of Illinois, who studied more than 200 Hopewell sites.

(continued)

© 1997 J. Weston Walch, Publisher   4   *Native Americans:*
A Thematic Unit on Converging Cultures

Adena–Hopewell–Mississippian Cultures:
Exploding the Myth of Primitiveness *(continued)*

the largest pyramid in the Americas.

This pyramid is known today as Monk's Mound. It measures 102 feet high and covers 14 acres at its base. It is larger than the Great Pyramid of Giza, in Egypt. The top of the mound may have been used for religious ceremonies celebrating the sun.

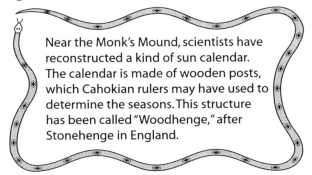

Near the Monk's Mound, scientists have reconstructed a kind of sun calendar. The calendar is made of wooden posts, which Cahokian rulers may have used to determine the seasons. This structure has been called "Woodhenge," after Stonehenge in England.

Around the city, hundreds of smaller mounds have been found. Many have been excavated and have been found to contain human remains and artifacts. Some Cahokian burials appear to be human sacrifices. These were carried out when an important figure died and his followers were killed to be interred with him. In one mass burial, archeologists found the remains of over 50 young women. Were they captives or relatives of the deceased? Did they go willingly to their deaths because of a strong belief in an afterlife? Scientists do not know. We do know that funerary customs and elaborate burials were an important part of Mississippian culture.

Explorers and Settlers Come to the Land

By the time European explorers first entered the American heartland, early in the

1500's, Cahokia was deserted. Vegetation had overgrown the mounds. What brought an end to this great urban center is not known. One possible explanation is disease, caused by poor sanitation. Another possibility is a change in the worldwide climate, beginning in the thirteenth century, which created lower temperatures. Other possibilities are overpopulation and depletion of food resources in the surrounding area, through overhunting and overfarming.

When the Europeans reached the land of the Mound Builders, they found only small, scattered bands of Indians. European settlers found it hard to identify these people with the remains of the great mounds. French Trappist monks built a monastery and garden on the great pyramid at Cahokia. Thus, it became known as the Monk's Mound. Later, farmers flattened mounds when they prepared their fields. Builders used the earth for fill. And looters plundered the mounds for burial remains. Only recently has the work of the Mound Builders been accepted as evidence of a highly advanced culture that flourished for hundreds of years before the first explorers penetrated the continent.

Glossary of Terms for This Unit:

pre-Columbian: Term used to designate America and its culture before Columbus arrived, in 1492 C.E.

obsidian: Volcanic glass, usually black in color, that can be sharpened into ideal cutting edges. Obsidian artifacts can be used for establishing historical dates because over time hydration (water) layers that can be measured form on their edges.

Comparing Cultures: Cahokia and Ancient Egypt

Directions: World history classes usually study the civilization of ancient Egypt but very rarely study Cahokia, the great culture of ancient North America. Fill out the following chart comparing ancient Egypt with Cahokia. Can you make a case for the study of Cahokia as a viable culture in the history of North America before European settlement?

	ANCIENT EGYPT	**CAHOKIA**
Dates for height of culture		
Geographic features		
Governmental organization		
Social structure		
Public buildings		
Writing system		
Funerary customs		
Craftsmanship		
Ways of making a living (farming? trade?)		
Religious beliefs		
Role of women		

To Excavate or Not? An Ethical Dilemma

One of the biggest issues facing archaeologists and anthropologists is whether to dig up ancient burial sites. Scientific study of skeletal remains can provide clues about how early peoples lived. Information about food, diseases, general health, and even appearance can be found. It is important to remember, however, that the remains are also ancestors. Many Native Americans believe that excavating burial sites is morally and ethically wrong. How can we meet the needs of science and still treat human remains with dignity and respect?

In this activity, you will take a role in an imaginary court case. The case is *Illinois Tribal Council* v. *American University of Archaeology.* The tribal council is suing the university to prevent ancient burial sites from being excavated. The university wants staff and students to be able to dig at and study the sites. Although this is not a real case, it can bring out concerns of the parties involved.

Roles	
anthropologist	graduate student in Native American history
archaeologist specializing in Native American artifacts	lawyers for prosecution and defense
graduate student in archaeology writing a dissertation on Indian mounds	judge
head of the Illinois Tribal Council	jurors, including a jury foreperson
tribal historian	other witnesses (for prosecution or defense) —writers, historians, medical specialists

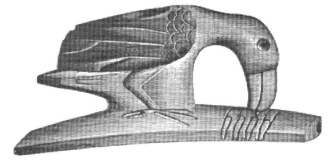

Carved bird pipe found in burial mound

Name _____

Date _____

A Page from the Past _____

The Mystery of the Mounds

When European settlers first came to the lands previously inhabited by the Mound Builders, they were astounded by the huge earthen structures they found. Theories on who built the mounds included many groups—Vikings, Egyptians, Phoenicians, Welsh, even the Ten Lost Tribes of Israel. Few people thought that Native Americans had been capable of such an achievement. The most popular theory was that the Mound Builders were a civilization that predated the Amerindians and were destroyed by the barbarous tribes who moved into the area later.

Interest in the mounds— their purpose, method of construction, and contents—fostered the growth of archaeology in America. Many amateur excavators delved into the mysterious mounds. Even Thomas Jefferson excavated a small mound near his home, in Virginia. Jefferson believed that the mounds were built by American Indians; but he was in the minority. Throughout the nineteenth century, the myth remained that Native Americans were not "advanced" enough to have constructed the mounds. In 1873, J.W. Foster, president of the Chicago Academy of Sciences, wrote that to suppose that Indians had created the mounds "is as preposterous, almost, as to suppose that they built the pyramids of Egypt."*

Finally, in 1881, John Welsey Powell, working for the Smithsonian Institution, authorized and funded an extensive survey of over 2,000 mounds in 24 states. The Smithsonian's final report, in 1894, stated that the myth of the Mound Builders as a separate race should not be accepted, that the Mound Builders and Native Americans were one and the same.

One part of the mystery was solved, but how and why the mounds were constructed is still being examined today. For example, one of the most puzzling structures is the Great Serpent Mound, in southern Ohio. This giant earthen sculpture is in the shape of a coiled snake swallowing what appears to be an egg. It is 1,254 feet long, 24 feet wide, and 5 feet high. This mound was not used for burials, so its purpose is unknown. A huge complex of Hopewell earthworks near Newark, Ohio, contains many different geometric structures and shapes. Estimates are that it took 300 years to build. Like the Serpent Mound, the function of this elaborate complex is not clear.

Other mounds—known burial sites— contained thousands of artifacts. Pearls, shells, shell beads, copper jewelry, clay pipes, animal effigies, axes, and knives are just a few of the items found in these burial mounds. Like the ancient Egyptians, the Mound Builders may have believed that their belongings would be useful in the afterlife. Some historians also believe that it was a liking for display and signs of ownership that motivated the Mound Builders to place so many objects in their graves.

After centuries of destruction and looting, most of the remaining mounds are now protected and preserved. In the 1890's, a director of Harvard University's Peabody Museum raised money from private citizens in Boston to preserve the Great Serpent Mound. In 1900, Harvard donated the site to the state of Ohio, which made it a state historical park. The site of Cahokia has been taken over by the state of Illinois, which maintains it and has built an interpretive museum near Monk's Mound. Many people today are fortunate to be able to visit these mounds and learn about the achievements of the early Americans who created such impressive structures.

---

* *Mound Builders and Cliffdwellers* (Alexandria, Virginia: Time-Life, 1992)

2. The Arctic Amerindians and Early Contact with Europe

Eskimo mask representing a being believed to control the supply of game

The Arctic Amerindians and Early Contact with Europe: Myth and Mystery

The scientific and historical study of the arctic north is challenging due to the harsh climate. Artifacts and organic materials alike are difficult to find, but when remains are found, sometimes they are amazingly well preserved. A good example is the bodies of seamen on the ill-fated 1845 Franklin expedition to find the Northwest Passage, which were found almost perfectly preserved in the permafrost. Autopsies showed an abnormal amount of lead in the sailors' remains, which led scientists to conclude that lead poisoning from canned goods might have contributed to the death of expedition members from exposure and starvation.

It is commonly believed that the Arctic may be where the first contact between Native Americans and Europeans took place, as early as 1000 C.E. Some scientists think that even earlier a transpolar culture may have regularly traveled back and forth from Europe to the Americas. Also, a mysterious people, sometimes called the Maritime Archaics, may have developed significant sailing skills, enough to use prevailing currents and winds to cross the northern Atlantic, bringing their culture from the arctic regions of North America to northern Europe—a dramatic departure from the customary explanation of who "discovered" whom. This "great northern route," the shortest distance between North America and Europe, is still followed today by aircraft and ships alike.

The search for the fabled Northwest Passage to the Pacific Ocean also made the Far North a place for exploration and interaction. Almost from the beginning of European contact with North America, explorers searched northern rivers and bays for some sort of passageway through the continent—a route to the Orient. Henry Hudson hoped that it might be the Hudson River, and Jacques Cartier searched for a passage in the Saint Lawrence River and Great Lakes region. When no passage was found in more temperate zones, only the Arctic remained to investigate for the elusive northern gateway to Asia.

Preparation for This Unit

This unit lends itself to examining motivations for exploration and expansion. Why would anyone want to explore the Arctic, risking such dangerous conditions? What were the explorers looking for? What resources could arctic and subarctic areas hold that would be valuable to Europeans? Why would anyone settle in such a harsh environment? Native Americans, who were extraordinarily adept at adapting to various environments, here thrived in an environment that to us appears incapable of supporting human life.

Student Activities

Worksheet 1 is a research project that asks students to separate myth from reality. Many groups claim to have "discovered" America first. What is the proof for each claim? Is the evidence artifactual or based on legend? Is it conceivable that these explorers could have reached the Western Hemisphere? Students use critical thinking skills to evaluate the probability.

Worksheet 2 is a map activity that lays the groundwork for studying different Native American culture groups and their contact with different European exploring and colonizing nations. You might wish to expand this activity to include the Native American tribes in your locality. Which European nations sent explorers to your area? Who claimed it first?

Eskimo mask of a human face

The Arctic Amerindians and Early Contact with Europe: Myth and Mystery

The arctic and subarctic regions have always fascinated people of the modern age. How do people adapt to such a harsh environment? How do they survive in conditions that seem incapable of supporting human life? These questions have been the subject of research, study, and speculation.

The people of the Far North also present us with some mysteries. The Eskimo peoples were the last **Amerindians** to arrive on the American continents. It is believed that earlier people preceded them. Scientists are still trying to discover who these early people were. It is probable that the first contact between Europeans and Native Americans occurred in the Far North, along the coast of Canada. When and how did this contact occur? Were there any lasting results? Archaeologists and historians are still investigating to learn if there was more communication between Eastern and Western Hemispheres than previously believed.

The Environment

Eskimo woman and child

The area known as the Arctic stretches across the top of the world. It includes the northern parts of Alaska, Canada, Siberia, and Greenland. It is a land of little or no vegetation due to the extreme cold. Winters are long and dark, and summers are very short. The sun may never set at the height of an arctic summer. The **indigenous** people depended totally upon animals for their food, clothing, tools, and even fuel. Few of the people we call Eskimos actually lived in the Arctic. Perhaps only about 10 percent of the total population lived there. Most lived in the subarctic, an area of conifer forests and rivers in southern Alaska and the interior of Canada. Wherever they lived, all of these people were alike in how they used the resources their environment provided. They all shared hunting techniques that enabled them to subsist totally on wild animals and fish.

Indian Culture Before the Arrival of Europeans

The Eskimos probably crossed from Asia to North America in boats. For when they came, the Bering Strait land bridge was underwater. It had been submerged as the ice caps shrank and the sea level rose during the last Ice Age. The genes of the Eskimos are more like those of the Asians than other Native American groups. Even though all arctic peoples are often called "Eskimo," this is an artificial name. There are several language groups among the northern people. *Eskimo* is not a word recognized in any of them. *Eskimo* probably originated from an Algonquian word that referred to snowshoes.

Their physical characteristics helped the Eskimo adapt to the cold. They tended to be stocky and compact, with fewer sweat glands, short limbs, and a high metabolism. These features helped them maintain body heat and survive the cold. Their diet also reflected their environment. The Inuit, Eskimos of the far north polar regions, subsisted almost totally on

(continued)

© 1997 J. Weston Walch, Publisher

12

Native Americans:
A Thematic Unit on Converging Cultures

The Arctic Amerindians and Early Contact
with Europe: Myth and Mystery *(continued)*

meat. They particularly relied on meat with a high fat content, such as whale blubber. They supplemented this diet with some fish and seabirds. However, caribou, walrus, seal, whale, and polar bear provided them with all the nutrients for survival.

The Eskimo were skillful hunters. They knew the habits and movements of all of the arctic animals. Whales, particularly the narwhal and beluga, migrated yearly into arctic waters. Eskimos hunted for whale in boats. They used one- or two-man kayaks or the larger umiaks. They harpooned the whales and dragged the carcasses ashore. Seal was probably the most important staple food for Eskimos living near the coast or on the pack ice. Hunters stalked the seal by moving near breathing holes in the ice. There, the seal would emerge every 15 to 20 minutes for air.

When the Eskimo made a kill, food was shared with the entire village. Eskimos believed that a wild animal did not belong to any individual. They also believed that it was an honor to share.

Animals were essential for clothing. Clothing was made of tanned skins. The skins were sewn by women using bone or ivory needles with thread made from beluga or caribou sinew. Caribou skins were most commonly used. In the winter, most Eskimos wore two sets of clothes. The inner layer had fur closest to the body. The outer layer had fur facing outward. A hood lined with wolf or wolverine fur protected the head and face. Seal hunters also wore an outer parka made of long strips of seal intestines sewn together. This waterproof garment was as effective as fabrics used for skiing outerwear today.

Eskimo dwellings changed with the season and the location of the group. In the summer, they were tents constructed of animal skins and pieces of driftwood and bone. Winter shelters were more substantial and permanent. Usually they were *not* the houses made of snow or ice that we picture. Most Eskimo winter dwellings were dug into the ground. They resembled earthen domes. A long, low entrance tunnel kept cold air out. The inner doorway was hung with skins to further reduce drafts. A small ceiling hole provided ventilation. A skylight made from a sheet of ice or from seal or walrus gut let in light. In coastal dwellings, oil produced from seal, whale, or walrus blubber was used as heating fuel. Interior temperatures were kept as high as 90 degrees Fahrenheit. Inland homes had to depend on such things as caribou fat and fish oil for their lamps. Plant material was used as fuel for cooking. Igloos were usually built only as temporary shelters. However, a few Eskimo who hunted in the Far North spent the entire winter in these snow houses.

Man's coat made of caribou hide

(continued)

Native Americans:
A Thematic Unit on Converging Cultures

The Arctic Amerindians and Early Contact with Europe: Myth and Mystery *(continued)*

Explorers and Settlers Come to the Land

The first contact between American Indians and Europeans probably occurred when Viking explorers met the Beothuk tribe in Newfoundland around 1000 C.E. The Vikings, or Norsemen, originated in the Scandinavian countries. They were a great seafaring people. They had already discovered and settled Iceland and Greenland earlier, in the tenth century. Norse sagas, ancient stories passed by word of mouth and then later written down, tell of the voyages of Leif Eriksson. Eriksson sailed from Greenland to a land he called Vinland. We now believe Vinland was Newfoundland. His voyage predates Columbus's arrival by almost 500 years.

Archaeological digs at L'Anse aux Meadows, Newfoundland, in the 1960's, proved that Vikings had built a settlement there. The settlement, which lasted only a few years, included substantial stone houses and a forge to smelt iron. Artifacts show that men and women lived at this site. That implies the site was meant to be permanent rather than temporary.
At L'Anse aux Meadows, the Vikings came into contact with the Beothuk. The Vikings called this subarctic tribe *Skraelings*, or barbarians. The Vikings traded with the Beothuk. They appear to have fought with them as well. These clashes likely led the Norse to abandon their site and return to Greenland. L'Anse aux Meadows was named a **World Heritage Site** in 1978. It is also a National Historic Site of Canada.

Eventually, the Norse also left the Viking sites in Greenland. Eskimos had moved into Greenland in the twelfth century. As time went on, suspicion and distrust resulted in violent confrontations between the Norsemen and the

Eskimo. Then the climate changed during the fourteenth century. Greenland become colder. The Norse livestock could not tolerate the temperature drop. By 1500, Norse settlements in Greenland were in ruins. Only the Eskimo remained. This may be the only time in history when native people remained as victors and Europeans were driven out.

Within a hundred years after the Norse left North America, other Europeans established contact with the natives of the Far North. This time, the Europeans were not looking for a place to settle. They were searching for the Northwest Passage—a waterway across the continent, connecting the Atlantic Ocean to the Pacific Ocean, giving easy access to Asia. Earlier expeditions in more temperate regions along the East Coast had failed. Thus, some explorers turned north to find a route.

In 1576, Martin Frobisher, an English sea captain, sailed into a large bay south of Baffin Island. Frobisher hoped the bay was the opening to the Northwest Passage. His relationship with the Eskimo was not without conflict. Five of his men disappeared. They were thought to have been captured by the Eskimo. In turn, Frobisher captured some Eskimos to take back to Europe. Unable to find a passageway to Asia, Frobisher tried to make his fortune another way. He took 200 pounds of ore back to England. He was sure the ore was gold. The ore was worthless, and he never found the Northwest Passage. In three trips to the Arctic, Frobisher succeeded only in alienating the native peoples.

The fate of his five missing crewmen was learned years later. Eskimos revealed that the five were released. The crewmen refused to wait for the Europeans to return. They built a boat

(continued)
Native Americans:
A Thematic Unit on Converging Cultures

© 1997 J. Weston Walch, Publisher

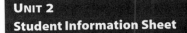

The Arctic Amerindians and Early Contact
with Europe: Myth and Mystery *(continued)*

from some timbers left by Frobisher. Then they sailed off, never to be seen again.

Other European voyages searched for the Northwest Passage. Many ended in tragedy. They were brought down by harsh conditions for which Europeans were unprepared. In 1610, Henry Hudson sailed into the bay that was later named for him. His ship became trapped in the ice. The crew was forced to spend the winter in Hudson Bay. The next summer, the crew mutinied. They cast Hudson, his son, and seven other people adrift in a small boat. The nine were never seen again. It was a sad end to an illustrious career of exploration.

Hudson Bay proved to be a dead end for explorers seeking passage to the Pacific. Merchants, however, found that it was an ideal spot for fur trading. In 1670, Hudson's Bay Company was established as a trading post with a charter from the king of England. Fur trade became very important in the north.

Even into the nineteenth century, explorers tried to find a route through the Arctic to the Pacific. The Franklin expedition of 1845 met with disaster. The ships became icebound. Crew members tried to cross the continent on foot. One hundred and thirty men perished from starvation. The remains of some of Franklin's men were found frozen in the permafrost. Autopsies showed evidence of lead poisoning from food stored in tin cans. Brain damage from lead poisoning could have caused the crew to make bad decisions. Thus, the venture may have been doomed to failure from the beginning.

Aftermath

Because of the harsh conditions of the Arctic, native peoples there were less affected by European contact than were the Amerindians who lived in more hospitable climates. The Eskimos were able to maintain their traditions and customs. Eventually, they, too, suffered from diseases brought by the traders. They also found their way of life threatened by new technologies. For example, steam-powered American whalers in the nineteenth and early twentieth centuries depleted the whale population. Whaling became much more difficult for the Eskimos. What about the Northwest Passage? In the late 1950's, a nuclear-powered submarine found a passageway to the Pacific when it crossed *under* the polar ice cap.

——— Glossary of Terms for This Unit———

Amerindian: One of many anthropological terms used to describe the original inhabitants of the American continents.

indigenous: People, plants, or animals original to a particular area.

World Heritage Site: A site designated by UNESCO (The United Nations Educational, Scientific, and Cultural Organization) as having significance in the development of world culture and history. Cahokia, in Illinois, is also a World Heritage Site.

Eskimo ivory carving half whale, half white bear

© 1997 J. Weston Walch, Publisher

Native Americans:
A Thematic Unit on Converging Cultures

Who Really "Discovered" America?

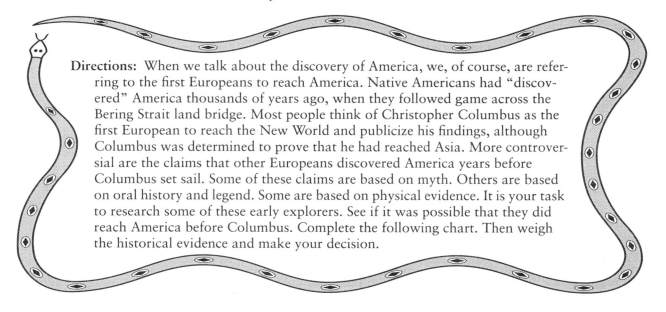

Directions: When we talk about the discovery of America, we, of course, are referring to the first Europeans to reach America. Native Americans had "discovered" America thousands of years ago, when they followed game across the Bering Strait land bridge. Most people think of Christopher Columbus as the first European to reach the New World and publicize his findings, although Columbus was determined to prove that he had reached Asia. More controversial are the claims that other Europeans discovered America years before Columbus set sail. Some of these claims are based on myth. Others are based on oral history and legend. Some are based on physical evidence. It is your task to research some of these early explorers. See if it was possible that they did reach America before Columbus. Complete the following chart. Then weigh the historical evidence and make your decision.

Explorer	Date	Landfall	Type of Seagoing Craft	Historical Evidence	Probability of Discovery (my opinion)
Saint Brendan					
Prince Madog (Madoc) Gwynedd of Wales					
The Chinese (Hui-Shen)					
The Egyptians					
The Phoenicians					
Leif Eriksson					
(Bonus) Henry Sinclair of Scotland					
Others?					

Cultures in Convergence

Directions: The outline map of North America on page 16 shows the areas claimed by European nations during the age of exploration and colonization. Below is a list of some major Native American tribes. With which European power did each tribe have the most contact (and often conflict)?

1. Wampanoag _____

2. Cherokee _____

3. Pueblo _____

4. Huron _____

5. Lakota _____

6. Tlingit _____

7. Calusa _____

8. Yani _____

9. Powhatan _____

10. Fox _____

Extra Challenge: Label the homeland of each tribe on the outline map.

© 1997 J. Weston Walch, Publisher

Native Americans:
A Thematic Unit on Converging Cultures

Cultures in Convergence *(continued)*

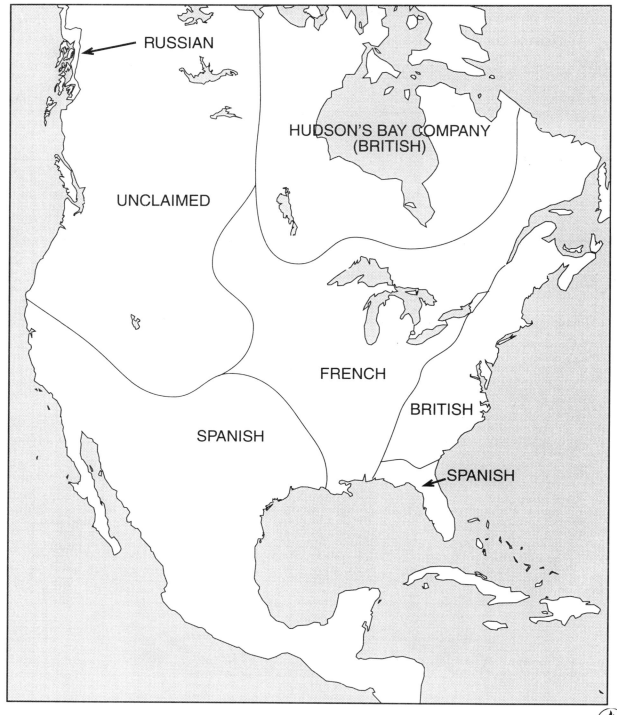

Native Americans:
A Thematic Unit on Converging Cultures

A Page from the Past

Russians in America

Perhaps the least known of the contacts between Europeans and Native Americans is that of the Russians and their dealing with the Aleuts and other Native Americans of the Pacific Northwest and Alaska. In 1728, Tsar Peter the Great, of Russia, sent the Danish sailor Vitus Bering to the Pacific Coast of Siberia to lead an expedition of discovery. The pursuit of furs was the goal of this expedition. The wealth that Siberian furs had brought to Russia provided the Russians' impetus to expand their trading area.

In 1741, Bering reached the Aleutian islands off the coast of Alaska and encountered the Aleuts. The Aleuts were great sea hunters and used skin-covered kayaks to hunt seal, walrus, and sea otter. They wore nose pendants, had tattoos, and dressed in waterproof parkas made of bird skins, with the down side worn inward. The Russians made fun of the Aleuts' appearance, but they respected their skill as hunters.

Determined to gain a profit in the fur trade, the Russians were very aggressive and brutal. They captured Aleut women and children and used them as hostages to force Aleut men to hunt sea otter for them. The Russians then traded the otter pelts to the Chinese, who especially valued the dark, lustrous fur.

The Russians established permanent settlements on Kodiak Island and on the Alaskan coast. As the Russian-American Company moved southward down the Gulf of Alaska, they encountered more organized resistance from the Native American tribes, such as the Tlingit. These tribes were strong enough to demand fair value for their furs and to resist Russian domination. In 1801, Tlingit warriors attacked a Russian trading outpost at Sitka. The Russians were able to recapture the area, but they were more careful in the future about establishing good relations with the Tlingit. English and American traders eventually pushed into this area and competed with the Russians. In reaction to this and to bolster their claims to the Pacific Coast, the Russians established bases in northern California as far south as the Russian River, in the Sonoma Valley. In 1812, the Russians founded Fort Ross, which was the only non-Hispanic settlement in the early history of California.

After the sea otter was hunted nearly to extinction, the Russians turned to other furs. Later, their interest dwindled as the influence of traders from England and America grew. In 1867, Russia sold Alaska with its unknown (at the time) wealth in gold and oil to the United States for $7.2 million dollars.

Tlingit drum with whale design

3. Indian Cultures of the Southwest Meet the Spanish Conquistadors

Basketwork shield from cliff-dwelling ancestors of the Pueblo

Indian Cultures of the Southwest Meet the Spanish Conquistadors

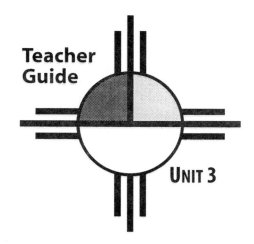

Of all the encounters between the native peoples of the Americas and European newcomers, none was more devastating than the first major contact—that between the indigenous people and the Spanish. Spain had just spent hundreds of years fighting the Muslims in the Iberian Peninsula; the last Moorish stronghold was defeated in 1492. The constant warfare of this *reconquista* fostered a warrior society, used to bloodshed and cruelty. So grievous was the Spanish treatment of native people in the New World, that the northern European states spread the Black Legend. According to the Black Legend, the downfall of Spain as a world power, beginning with England's defeat of the Spanish Armada in 1588, was explained by Spain's evil policies in the Americas. Northern European propagandists claimed that God was punishing Spain for its sins, despite the fact that other European powers meted out equally harsh treatment to native people.

This unit examines some of the initial contacts between the Spanish conquistadors and the indigenous people of North America, particularly in the Southwest, focusing on the Pueblo peoples of what is today New Mexico through the Pueblo Revolt of 1680.

Preparation for This Unit

A background understanding of European history would be helpful here. Perhaps an overview of the Renaissance and Reformation might help students grasp the many forces that inter-

acted to encourage European nations to explore and expand outside their borders. Because of the 1992 Quincentennial, there are abundant current materials about Columbus, Spanish motivations for exploration, and the human and ecological toll of this initial contact between Europeans and Native Americans.

Student Activities

Worksheet 1 examines one dramatic outcome of contact between the Old World and the New—an interchange of plants and animals. Plants from the Americas, such as potatoes and corn, permanently altered the diet of people the world over. Domestic animals from the Old World brought ranching and farming to the New World and provided a stable source of meat as well as a means of transportation. They also brought some new problems. Cattle, pigs, and horses brought new diseases into the Americas that affected indigenous species, such as bison, and also competed with those species for food. Included is a list of food products from both hemispheres: Do not hand it out to students until they have completed the Great Food Exchange activity. They can then check their answers.

Worksheet 2 examines reasons for conquest in the Americas. Students are asked to evaluate Spain's major motives and rank them in order of importance. Both activities lend themselves well to group work.

Indian Cultures of the Southwest Meet the Spanish Conquistadors

In North America, the Native Americans of the Southeast and Southwest were the first to feel major impacts from contact with Europeans. They encountered Spanish explorers sent to claim territory for Spain and to search for treasures. The Mississippian culture of the Southeast (see Unit 1) was devastated by contact with the Spanish. But Pueblo Indians of the Southwest met the Spanish with enough resistance to preserve their culture.

The Pueblos were named by the Spanish for their well-constructed towns—"town" is *pueblo* in Spanish. The ancestors of the Pueblo people were the Anasazi. The Anasazi built elaborate cliff dwellings. Mesa Verde and Chaco Canyon are two examples. The Anasazi engaged in successful desert agriculture. Around 1300 C.E., they left the desert, perhaps due to a drought. Many settled in the Rio Grande Valley.

Shield of the Zuni priesthood

Indian Culture Before the Arrival of the Europeans

The Pueblos were a mixture of tribes with many languages. Their 80 or so settlements showed great individuality as well as some cultural similarities. They built houses of stone and **adobe**. Their houses were often very elaborate, with multiple levels. The Pueblos were experts at agriculture in a dry climate. Using irrigation, they cultivated corn, squash, and beans.

Religion was the most important part of Pueblo life. Each town was governed by religious societies. Priests supervised community affairs and oversaw religious ceremonies. In a society so dependent upon agriculture, the land was of great importance. Pueblo peoples, such as the Zuni, believed that the land was the Earth

Mother. They believed that it was controlled by sacred spirits called kachinas or katsinas. These spirits represented rain and plant growth and other natural forces. The people honored the spirits in ceremonies involving music and dance. Every member of the community took part in the ceremonies. In this way, they maintained a spiritual balance with nature. The Spanish conquistadors arrived in the sixteenth century and disrupted this world of ritual and ceremony.

Explorers and Settlers Come to the Land

The Spanish were the first Europeans to explore what is now the United States. Based upon the voyages of Christopher Columbus (1492–1504), they conquered the islands of the Caribbean. Then they turned their attention to

(continued)

Indian Cultures of the Southwest Meet the Spanish Conquistadors *(continued)*

the north. In 1513, Juan Ponce de León landed on the North American mainland. He called the area La Florida, after the Eastertime feast of flowers. Ponce de León was looking for gold and the fabled fountain of youth. He failed to find either. He and his men were driven from the land by the native people, the Calusas.

The Spanish wanted this territory for strategic purposes—to keep out the French and British. Earlier explorers had found Florida barren of gold. But others remained unconvinced. In 1539, Hernando de Soto arrived on Florida's west coast. With him were 600 soldiers, 100 servants, 200 horses, a herd of pigs, and many huge attack dogs. De Soto had accompanied Pizarro to Peru. There, he had seen the gold and other riches of the Inca civilization that the Spanish had seized. He hoped to find similar wealth and glory in North America.

The expedition traveled through the American Southeast. De Soto's men plundered the rich Mississippian towns, captured Indians as slaves, and committed many atrocities. Thousands of Mobile tribe Indians died when the Spanish burned their town. The Spanish also unknowingly carried European diseases that soon killed thousands of native people. Native Americans had no immunity to European diseases. The result was what is called a **virgin soil epidemic**. De Soto's expedition journeyed to the Mississippi River. There de Soto died from an illness in 1542. The survivors reached Mexico a year later. The de Soto expedition resulted in near total destruction of the Amerindian cultures of the Southeast.

Meanwhile, the Spanish were eyeing territories west of the Mississippi River. In 1528, an ill-fated expedition led by Pánfilo de Narváez landed on the Florida coast. Beset by the

Apalachee Indians, the expedition fled by sea. Their ships were lost, one by one. Of 245 men, only 4 survived. The survivors were washed up on the Gulf Coast near present-day Galveston, Texas.

One of them was Spanish nobleman Álvar Núñez Cabeza de Vaca. Cabeza de Vaca led his fellow survivors across what is today the American Southwest. They tried to find the way to Mexico. Their exact route is unknown. But they probably were the first Europeans to enter the American West. Cabeza de Vaca survived among the native peoples by trading and by healing the sick. He and his companions finally reached a Spanish outpost in Mexico in 1536. They had been gone for nine years.

Cabeza de Vaca told the Spanish authorities that he had seen no wealth or riches. But he said that he had heard talk of seven fabulously wealthy cities farther to the north. The Spanish were eager to find the "Seven Cities of Gold." The first two explorers they sent were an African slave named Estéban, one of Cabeza de Vaca's three companions, and a **Franciscan friar** named Marcos. Estéban was killed by the Zuni. Marcos returned saying that the Zuni pueblo Hawikuh was magnificent. He said that it was encrusted with jewels and that it was only the smallest of the seven lost cities. The viceroy of Mexico decided to send an expedition. He chose Francisco Vásquez de Coronado to explore the region and to take it for Spain. In 1540, Coronado set out with over 200 mounted soldiers, 1,000 Mexican Indians, and herds of sheep, cattle, and horses.

After four months, Coronado reached the Zuni village. He found no evidence of fabulous riches. The

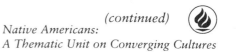

24

(continued)
Native Americans:
A Thematic Unit on Converging Cultures

Indian Cultures of the Southwest Meet the Spanish Conquistadors *(continued)*

Routes of Spanish Explorers

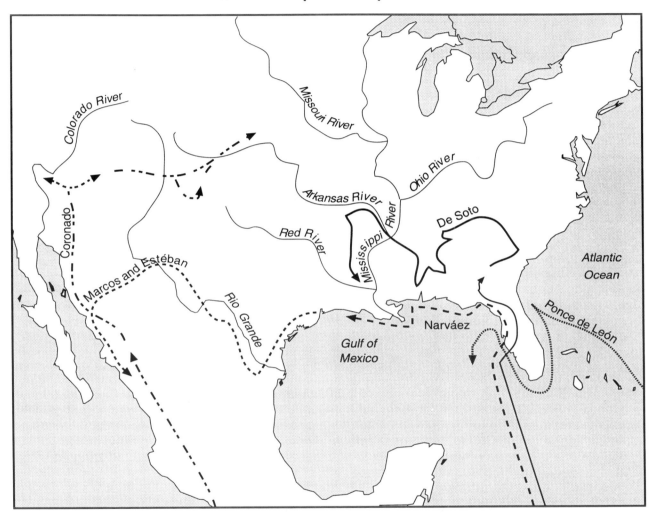

Early Spanish Explorations

◄ – – – – Coronado 1540–1542   ◄ - - - - - - - Marcos and Estéban

◄———— De Soto 1539–1542   ◄·············· Ponce de León

(continued)
Native Americans:
A Thematic Unit on Converging Cultures

Indian Cultures of the Southwest Meet the Spanish Conquistadors *(continued)*

native people were unmoved by demands that they surrender to Spain and adopt Christianity. They refused to open their town to Coronado's forces. A battle ensued. Zuni arrows were no match for Spanish guns and horses. Coronado entered the town. He seized the Zuni food storehouse to feed his expedition.

From Hawikuh, Coronado went on to other villages. He had to face the same reality: There was no treasure. The Spanish troops abused Pueblo women, allowed their herds to destroy Indian crops, and emptied the food supplies. Desperate for riches to justify his expedition, Coronado followed a Pawnee Indian onto the Great Plains. They went as far north as Kansas in search of a wealthy kingdom called Quivira. This, too, proved to be a myth. Coronado gave up and returned to Mexico. His expedition was a failure for Spain. It was a disaster for the Pueblo. Their valuable food stores were destroyed, hundreds of their people were killed, and many of their towns were burned.

After Coronado's expedition, the Spanish government ignored the Pueblo people for over half a century. Reeling from Coronado's visit and the diseases that it had spread, the Pueblo towns tried to stabilize their lives. In 1598, Don Juan de Oñate, one of the wealthiest men in Mexico, was appointed governor of the Pueblo lands. He arrived with 400 people. They included 130 families, Franciscan priests, and Mexican Indian servants. With them were many thousand head of livestock. In the upper valley of the Rio Grande, Oñate ordered the Tewa people to turn over one of their towns to the colonists. The town was renamed San Juan. The Spanish built a church and sent out priests to convert Native Americans to Christianity.

The Pueblo religion and the Catholicism brought by the Franciscans had certain similarities. Both had a sacred place to worship. The Spanish worshiped in a church. The Pueblos worshiped in a *kiva*, an underground, cavelike chamber. Both had elaborate ceremonies and rituals. But the difference between Catholicism and the Pueblo religion provoked Spanish intolerance and persecution. Pueblos believed in many spirits instead of one Supreme Being. Rather than heaven and hell, they believed that all people went to the same afterworld to live much as they had on earth. They put no emphasis on sin and atonement, as Catholicism did. The priests did not attempt to understand the Indians' traditional beliefs. They saw them only as barbaric and unacceptable. Converting the Pueblo to Catholicism became essential.

Pueblos who resisted faced reprisal. When the people of Acoma attacked a Spanish force, Oñate burned the village. Hundreds of natives were killed or sentenced to 20 years of labor. Every surviving man over the age of 25 was sentenced to public mutilation by having one foot cut off. Instead of repressing the Pueblo, this violence stirred them to rebel. Disgusted and discouraged, many of the original Spanish colonists returned to Mexico. Eventually, in 1606, Oñate was recalled and charged with mismanagement.

The Spanish did not give up on colonizing the land of the Pueblos. They sent new officials and more missionaries and established a new capital city called Santa Fe, in 1610. For years, the Pueblo were forced to convert to Catholicism. They also had to contribute labor and resources to the Spanish colonists. From time to time, individual Pueblo settlements rose in revolt. Finally, in 1680, a unified rebellion under

(continued)
Native Americans:
A Thematic Unit on Converging Cultures

Indian Cultures of the Southwest Meet the Spanish Conquistadors *(continued)*

Site of Acoma, village burned in reprisal

native religious leaders drove the Spanish out of Pueblo lands for 12 years. When the Spanish returned in 1692, they treated the native peoples better and were more tolerant of their religious beliefs. By the beginning of the eighteenth century, Spanish colonists needed the Pueblo people for fighting raiding tribes, such as the Apache, and for protecting Spanish territory from other European powers.

Because of their strong resistance, the Pueblos continued a way of life that remained relatively intact into the twentieth century.

——— Glossary of Terms for This Unit ———

adobe: Sun-dried brick.

Franciscan friar: A member of a religious order of the Roman Catholic Church, founded in the thirteenth century by St. Francis of Assisi and noted for missionary activities.

virgin soil epidemic: An outbreak of disease that occurs in a location where its microbes have never existed before, and therefore where people have not acquired immunities to the disease.

The Great Food Exchange!

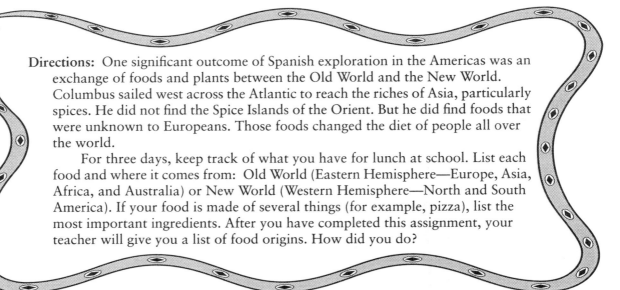

Directions: One significant outcome of Spanish exploration in the Americas was an exchange of foods and plants between the Old World and the New World. Columbus sailed west across the Atlantic to reach the riches of Asia, particularly spices. He did not find the Spice Islands of the Orient. But he did find foods that were unknown to Europeans. Those foods changed the diet of people all over the world.

For three days, keep track of what you have for lunch at school. List each food and where it comes from: Old World (Eastern Hemisphere—Europe, Asia, Africa, and Australia) or New World (Western Hemisphere—North and South America). If your food is made of several things (for example, pizza), list the most important ingredients. After you have completed this assignment, your teacher will give you a list of food origins. How did you do?

Lunch Food	Old World or New World?

(continued)

The Great Food Exchange! *(continued)*

New World	Old World
corn	wheat
potato	Asian rice
tomato	barley, oats, soybeans
peppers (red, green, yellow)	sugarcane
beans (lima, pole, navy, kidney)	onion
pumpkin	lettuce
squash	watermelon
cassava root (manioc or tapioca)	peach
avocado	pear
zucchini	apple
peanut, cashew, pecan	citrus fruits
pineapple	banana
yam	olive
blueberry	wine grape
sunflower	dandelion
gum (chicle latex)	cattle
tobacco	pigs
quinine	sheep
chocolate	chickens
vanilla	honeybees
turkey	coffee

Gold, God, and Glory?

Directions: Spanish motives for conquest and exploration of the New World are usually categorized under three headings: Gold, God, and Glory. To examine these major motivations, give examples of each. Then rank the "three G's" in order of their importance in Spain's decisions about how to govern its New World territories. Be prepared to defend your conclusions.

Gold

_____

_____

_____

_____

_____

God

_____

_____

_____

_____

_____

Glory

_____

_____

_____

_____

_____

A Page from the Past

Old World Animals in the New World

We take it for granted that Old MacDonald might have horses, sheep, cows, and pigs on his famous farm. But these animals did not exist in the Americas before the first Spanish explorers and settlers arrived. One significant effect of European conquest of the New World was an interchange of plants and animals between the Eastern and Western Hemispheres. The ancestors of our common domestic farm animals were brought to America from Europe.

Horses existed in the Americas in prehistoric times. But for some reason, the species became extinct. Columbus brought horses with him on his second voyage, in 1493. It took some time for them to become established in any great numbers in the New World. Despite their size, horses are not that hardy. They are susceptible to disease and are picky eaters. Many died on shipboard during the crossing. In the New World, the survivors did not adapt well to the tropical environment of the West Indies, where the first Spanish settlements were located. By contrast, when horses were brought to the grasslands of North America, they flourished. They became an essential part of the life of the Plains Indian tribes.

Cattle came from Spain, as early as 1493. These early breeds were lean and tough. They were adaptable and able to forage for food, even in the hot, moist climate of the West Indies. In 1521, Hernán Cortés brought cattle to Mexico. Cattle ranches were soon established to provide beef for the Spanish settlers. Cattle supplied not only meat, but also power in the New World. On the sugar-growing islands of the West Indies, they were used to haul sugarcane and to turn the shafts that operated the sugar mills. Cattle adapted well to the New World. Cows often produced two or three calves a year. In the seventeenth century, ranches were established in what is now Texas. And the Texas longhorn was developed on mission-run ranches by selective breeding. The huge herds of cattle associated with American cowboys started with those few cattle brought from Spain in the fifteenth century.

Probably no animal imported from the Old World had as much of an ecological impact as the pig. The mainstays of the Spanish diet were bread, olive oil, wine, and pork or beef. The conquistadors wanted familiar foods. So, large numbers of pigs were transported from Spain. As Spanish explorers moved through the new land, they drove herds of pigs along the route to provide fresh meat. Like horses and cattle, pigs arrived as early as 1493. They proved to be much more adaptable than other livestock. Their reproduction rate was 6 times that of cattle and 12 times that of horses. And the pigs were true omnivores—they ate just about anything.

Pigs escaped into the jungles of the West Indies and changed the flora and fauna of the islands immeasurably. They rooted up staples of the native diet, such as sweet potato and manioc tubers. They ate fruit. They killed lizards and baby birds for food. Everywhere pigs were introduced, they adapted and thrived. And they posed a serious challenge to plants and animals. In New England, pigs even ate shellfish from the tidal flats. As the Spanish moved into the American South and Southwest, pigs again escaped from captivity to become feral, or wild, animals. A few generations in the wild changed the tame porker of Europe into the wild hog, or razorback, in America. These lean, ferocious animals are often hunted as game in southern states. Their reputation for being tough and mean has earned them a place as mascot for the University of Arkansas sports teams.

A Page from the Past

Popé

On August 10, 1680, the Pueblo Indians of New Mexico rose in rebellion against Spain. It was probably the first and last time that Amerindians overthrew a powerful European presence. At the center of the Pueblo Revolt was a medicine man named Popé.

By 1680, the Spanish had controlled the American Southwest for 140 years. An important function of the Spanish colonies in the New World was to support the missionary activities of the Catholic Church. By 1626, Franciscan friars had converted 20,000 Indians to Christianity and had constructed 27 churches. The Franciscans were zealous in supporting Christianity and suppressing Pueblo religious beliefs. To further fuel the conflict between Spaniards and Native Americans, the royal governors of New Mexico drained the wealth of the province by stealing livestock and goods from Indian and settler alike. A drought in the 1660's and Europeans diseases also devastated the Pueblo Indians.

Many Pueblos turned back to their traditional beliefs, convinced that the Christian religion lacked the power to protect and sustain them. In 1675, the Spanish governor tried to prevent the return to the ancient beliefs. He arrested 47 Pueblo priests on charges of witchcraft and sorcery. In response, the Pueblos threatened to join the Apaches and the Navajo in an armed rebellion. The governor knew he was outnumbered. He released the medicine men, including Popé.

Popé was a middle-aged medicine man from Taos, about 50 miles north of the capital city of Santa Fe. He had resisted Christianity all his life. Captivity and harsh treatment by the Spanish fueled his hatred of their culture. Popé immediately began to plan a rebellion against the Spanish. Plans for the uprising were kept strictly secret. When Popé's son-in-law was suspected of being a spy for the Spanish,

Popé had him stoned to death as a lesson to other informers.

The rebellion was first set for August 11, 1680. It was moved up a day when it was feared that the Spanish had uncovered the plot. Bands of Indians killed missionaries and overran the haciendas, ranches of Spanish settlers. Despite a desperate fight by the Spanish forces, Santa Fe was evacuated. The Indians were victorious.

Although Popé's role in the fighting is not known, he soon exerted himself as a dictator. He dressed in elaborate robes. He was drawn through the streets in the former governor's carriage. Indians who had not joined the rebellion were enslaved.

Popé declared that "the God of the Christians is dead. He was made of rotten wood." Popé then proceeded to obliterate all vestiges of Christianity in Pueblo lands. He tore down churches. He forbade the use of Christian names. Indians who had been baptized were scrubbed clean with the seeds of the yucca plant to remove the "taint" of Christianity.

Popé was not content with removing the religion of Spain. He wanted to eliminate all aspects of European culture. No Spanish could be spoken. Plants from Spain—peaches, onions, melons, wheat, grapes, and citrus fruits—were uprooted. Only the traditional Pueblo crops of corn, beans, and squash could be grown. Livestock were slaughtered. Horses were set free from corrals. Many of these horses made their way north and west. There, they were captured by Plains Indians, which led to drastic changes in the Plains.

Popé had no more success than the Spanish in controlling the weather. Drought continued to take its toll on the Pueblo population. In 1688, Popé died, possibly murdered by his own people. In 1692, the Spanish regained control. The Pueblo Revolt was ended.

© 1997 J. Weston Walch, Publisher

Native Americans:
A Thematic Unit on Converging Cultures

4. Indian Cultures of the Great Lakes Region Meet the French Voyageurs

Birchbark patterns made by woodland tribes

Indian Cultures of the Great Lakes Region Meet the French Voyageurs

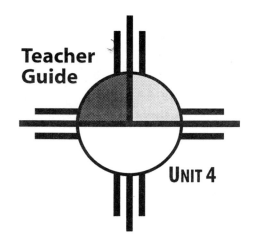

Studying the French in Canada and the Great Lakes region shows that indigenous Native American cultures were weakened by European contact even when relations between the two groups were fairly peaceful. Of all the Europeans in the New World, the French tried hardest to understand Native Americans and to adapt to their ways. Many French trappers married Amerindians. Their descendents, people of mixed French and Indian ancestry known as *métis*, were a unique and influential culture in a number of communities in the Great Lakes region and Canada.

Although the French had no wish to take over Indian lands and their plans for European settlements in America did not materialize, interaction with the French still disrupted Native American life on a massive scale. Disease, social disorder brought about by French trading and trade goods, and the introduction of Christianity into the native culture made intertribal disputes escalate into wars. Tribes moved or were displaced from their traditional lands. Some were so depleted by disease, war, or starvation that they barely remained viable as independent communities. Such was the case with the Hurons, the Native Americans who became the most important partners for the French in the fur trade.

The case study for this unit, the French and the Hurons, illustrates how despite the best mutual intentions, contact between disparate cultures disrupted and eventually destroyed the old way of life for native peoples.

————— **Preparation for this Unit** —————

Students would benefit from an overview of the geography of the Great Lakes region and of the great river systems of North America in preparation for this unit. Another interesting ancillary topic is the names of Native American tribes. Very few tribes are known by what they call themselves. The name that we know was usually given by European explorers, or even by another enemy tribe. For example, the Nez Percé were called that by the French because some of them pierced their noses. The Neutrals were a tribe between Lake Erie and Lake Ontario who remained neutral in disputes between the Hurons and the Iroquois. The Pequots owe their name, which means "the destroyers," to enemy tribes. Most Native American tribes either refer to themselves in their native language as "the people" or they name themselves in reference to their geographical location. Wampanoag means "people of the first light," since this tribe inhabited the coast of New England, where the sun rises first. Have your students investigate the origins of other Native American tribal names, for example, Delaware, Navajo, and Blackfoot.

─────── **Student Activities** ───────

Worksheet 1 involves French place-names. Sometimes contributions of the French *voyageurs* are overshadowed by our focus on the British. At one time the entire heartland of North America was part of France, which is evidenced by many French names and some additional cultural remnants. This activity is a good Internet research project. Many towns and cities have websites linked to the history of the area. Worksheet 2 examines how French and Native Americans mingled and interchanged cultures. Both peoples learned and borrowed more from one another than was the case in any other Native American/European contact.

Indian Cultures of the Great Lakes Region
Meet the French Voyageurs

One of Spain's rivals in the New World was France. The Spanish had frustrated French attempts to settle in the American Southeast. By the end of the sixteenth century, the French turned their attention to the region around the Great Lakes and what we know today as Canada. French claims in this area were based on the explorations of Jacques Cartier in the 1530's. Cartier sailed up the Saint Lawrence River in search of riches and the elusive Northwest Passage, the gateway to Asia. What France ultimately found in the New World was neither a route to the Orient nor the gold that the Spanish were so desperately seeking. France found something that proved to be as good as gold: furs. The Native Americans with whom the French had the most contact in their extensive fur trade were the Hurons.

Indian People Before the Arrival of the Europeans

The Hurons were an Iroquoian-speaking people whose name for themselves was *wendat*, "dwellers of the peninsula." They lived in an area of what is today Ontario, surrounded on three sides by water. The French called them Huron. The name came from the French word *hure*, meaning "boar's head," describing the men's bristly hairstyle (similar to what we call a Mohawk today). Huronia, the land occupied by the Hurons, contained about 25 villages. Population estimates for when the French arrived range between 20,000 and 40,000 Hurons.

The Hurons were farmers who supplemented agriculture with hunting. Over 80 percent of their diet was from such cultivated crops as

corn, squash, and beans. These three crops were so important to Native American groups that they are known as the "three sisters." The Hurons had extensive cornfields, with thousands of acres under cultivation. They produced so much corn that they were able to trade the surplus to other tribes. The Hurons' location was near the northern limit for corn cultivation. So, tribes farther north depended on them for this valuable food. The Hurons lived at the crossroads of the Great Lakes region (around modern-day Georgian Bay, in Ontario). Thus they were central to trading among the tribes of the area.

The Hurons were the dominant people in the area north of the Great Lakes. They consisted of eight **matrilineal** clans. Their government was on three levels: village, tribe, and confederation—a union of the four Huron tribes. All decisions were made by group consensus.

The long-standing rivals of the Hurons were the five tribes of the Iroquois Confederation, in what is today New York State. The Hurons and Iroquois warred almost constantly. The Iroquois were superior warriors and were able to capture prisoners. Many of the captured Hurons were adopted into the Iroquois tribes and accepted as full members of the community. In this way, the Iroquois managed to maintain their population. When disaster befell the Hurons in the seventeenth century, the Iroquois were unable to replace their tribal members with captive Hurons. Thus the Iroquois population dwindled to near extinction.

(continued)

Indian Cultures of the Great Lakes Region
Meet the French Voyageurs *(continued)*

Routes of French Explorers

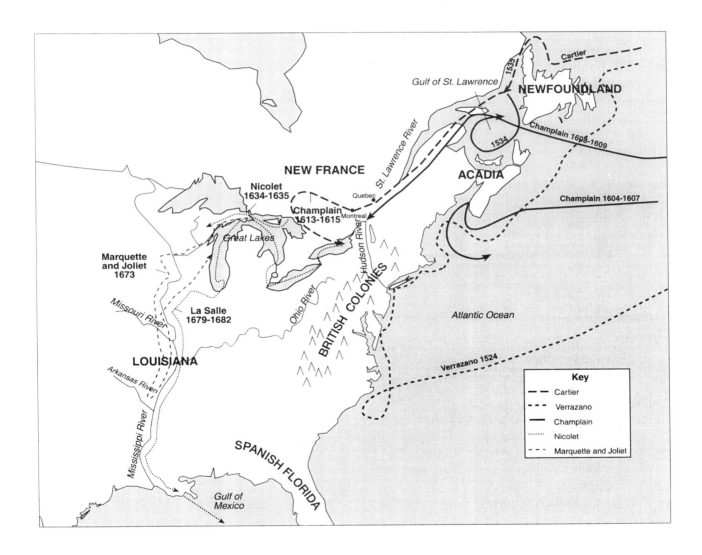

(continued)

Native Americans:
A Thematic Unit on Converging Cultures

Indian Cultures of the Great Lakes Region
Meet the French Voyageurs *(continued)*

Explorers and Settlers Come to the Land

Jacques Cartier sailed into the entrance of the Saint Lawrence River in 1534. He claimed the region for France. He found none of the gold and riches that the Spanish were plundering from Peru. But the French government felt that this region was worth further exploration. The hope was to find a shortcut to Asia. The next year, Cartier sailed farther up the Saint Lawrence. He established a settlement near the site of present-day Quebec City. An unexpectedly harsh northern winter nearly wiped out Cartier's men. Cartier returned to France. The French did not follow up their claims to the region for over 60 years. They were occupied with political and religious wars in Europe. By the late 1500's, Europeans began to establish relationships with the native people and to trade for furs.

Samuel de Champlain was the true founder of the French colonial effort in America. Champlain explored and mapped the coast of New England between 1604 and 1607. He turned north in 1608 to found the settlement of Quebec, on the Saint Lawrence. Hurons soon were visiting Quebec with canoeloads of furs to trade for French products. Beaver was the most valuable fur because it was thick and waterproof. But martin, lynx, and deer skins were also traded. In return, the French traded knives, axes, bright-colored cloth, and European foodstuffs. The Hurons tried to keep the French from going farther into the interior. They acted as middlemen between between the traders and inland tribes. Champlain did, however, travel to Lake Huron and Lake Ontario to search for an opening to the Pacific Ocean. He then sent his trusted follower Jean Nicolet to push farther west into the Great Lakes. Nicolet came prepared. He arrived at one Native American village dressed in a Chinese ceremonial robe and mandarin cap. He was certain he was close to the Orient at last and wished to appear properly dressed.

The lands that the French claimed did not attract large numbers of settlers. Therefore, trade became the basis for the French economy in North America. The French who did come to the New World were very different from the Spanish conquistadors of the Southwest. The French were few in number. And they depended on the Native Americans to supply furs. Thus, relations between the two groups were often cordial. French traders adopted Indian ways, learned native languages, and often married into the tribes. They wore the buckskin clothing of the Indians. And they used native inventions, such as the canoe and snowshoes.

Although they were friends, business associates, and relatives, the French unknowingly caused great distress to the native peoples. They brought diseases that spread into the American heartland along with the trade. The alliance that the French formed with the Hurons involved them in the long-standing conflict between the Great Lakes tribes and the Iroquois Confederation. Champlain made the Iroquois particularly angry by accompanying his Huron allies in battles against the Iroquois. Rivalries for furs developed among other European nations, including the English and the Dutch. Indian tribes were driven to hunt in territories not traditionally theirs. Competition for furs fueled intertribal conflicts and wars. Tribes were displaced from their homelands and pushed farther to the north and west.

(continued)

Indian Cultures of the Great Lakes Region
Meet the French Voyageurs *(continued)*

The Trapper's Bride, by Alfred Jacob Miller, 1850

Into this unstable situation came **Jesuits**. They were the missionaries who brought Catholicism to the Indians of **New France**. To establish Catholic communities, the Jesuits clustered the nomadic tribes together into settlements. In tribes with established villages, the missionaries lived among the Indians to gain acceptance. Despite their good intentions, the Jesuits often caused ideological splits within tribes. Those who accepted Christianity were separated from those who held to traditional beliefs. Also, bringing tribes together in concentrated communities made diseases spread more quickly among native peoples. Disease killed nearly half of the population of Huronia during the 1630's.

When epidemics struck, the Indians often blamed the missionaries. The Jesuits were not affected because, as Europeans, they were immune to many European diseases. Sometimes they were killed in reprisal. Sometimes they were captured, tortured, maimed, or executed by rival tribes. Despite this, the Jesuits persisted in their missionary work. Eventually, they spread into the North American interior, following the path of the explorers and traders.

Huronia was destroyed when the Iroquois went on the warpath. The Iroquois wanted to expand their hunting grounds and to take over the middleman's role in the fur trade. Their villages under attack, the Hurons fled to the French to seek protection. Jesuits settled the

(continued)

Native Americans:
A Thematic Unit on Converging Cultures

© 1997 J. Weston Walch, Publisher

39

Indian Cultures of the Great Lakes Region
Meet the French Voyageurs *(continued)*

Hurons on an island. But they failed to provide them with the necessary supplies for winter. Only 300 out of 6,000 Hurons survived.

Aftermath

The French traders lost their trading partners and depleted the fur-bearing animals in the Great Lakes region. Therefore, they began to move farther into the American interior in search of fur. The **coureurs de bois** moved into the north-central woodlands. The **voyageurs** traveled the inland waterways to find new trading prospects. French traders were not the only people on the move. Many Indian tribes fled from the hostile Iroquois. They abandoned their traditional homelands in what are now Ohio, Indiana, and Illinois.

To secure the interior, the French sent explorers. Among them were Father Jacques Marquette, a Jesuit missionary, and Louis Jolliet, in 1673. They explored the Mississippi River and the river systems which fed it. In 1682, René-Robert Cavelier, Sieur de la Salle, traveled the entire length of the Mississippi to the Gulf of Mexico. La Salle claimed the Mississippi and all of its tributaries for France. He named the territory Louisiana in honor of King Louis XIV.

In 1701, a peace treaty was signed in Montreal between the French and the Iroquois. But the fur trade had left its mark. Native peoples had developed a desire for European goods. These goods could only be had in trade for furs. Native Americans neglected their fields, stopped cultivating crops, and spent their time hunting and trapping. They came to depend more on trade with the Europeans, particularly for staples like flour and sugar. The native life

cycle—thousands of years of fishing, hunting, and planting crops—was undone. Unscrupulous traders introduced Indians to alcohol. They encouraged the Indians to binge, hoping that they would be easier to cheat. The worst tragedy of all was when an area was overhunted and overtrapped and, consequently, depleted of furs. The old way of life was gone. The new way of life was based on a resource that proved all too finite. When the furs ran out, many Indian tribes ceased to exist as viable communities.

The remnants of the once-mighty Hurons scattered. Some actually joined the Iroquois tribes. Some moved to Ohio and, eventually, on to Oklahoma. A few remained near Quebec City. Now known as the Wyandot, a name close to their original name, the Huron of Huronia did not survive contact with the European culture.

——— Glossary of Terms for This Unit ———

coureur de bois: Literally, "runner of woods." Someone who keeps to the woods, a French trader who concentrated on hunting and trading in the backwoods of North America.

Jesuits: The Society of Jesus. A highly disciplined order of the Roman Catholic Church, noted for educational activities.

matrilineal: A culture that traces the line of descent through women.

New France: The French colonies in continental North America.

voyageur: French trader who traveled great distances, usually by canoe, to trade for furs.

French Influence in the Heartland

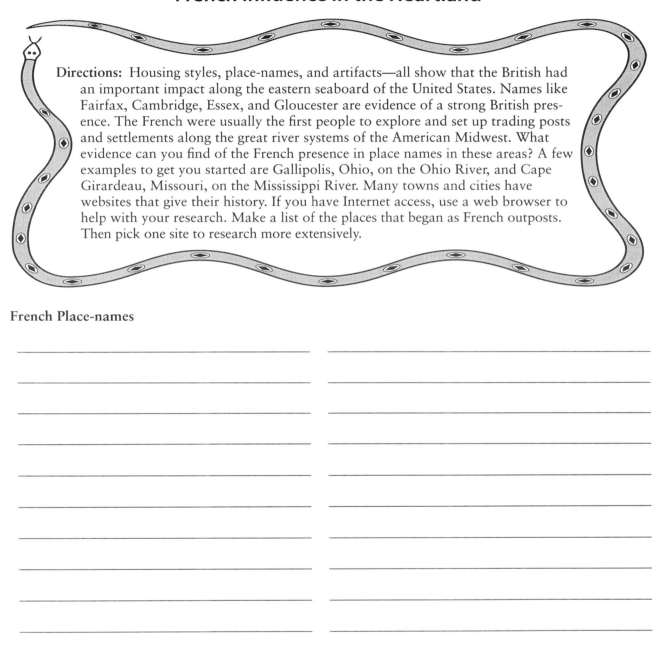

Directions: Housing styles, place-names, and artifacts—all show that the British had an important impact along the eastern seaboard of the United States. Names like Fairfax, Cambridge, Essex, and Gloucester are evidence of a strong British presence. The French were usually the first people to explore and set up trading posts and settlements along the great river systems of the American Midwest. What evidence can you find of the French presence in place names in these areas? A few examples to get you started are Gallipolis, Ohio, on the Ohio River, and Cape Girardeau, Missouri, on the Mississippi River. Many towns and cities have websites that give their history. If you have Internet access, use a web browser to help with your research. Make a list of the places that began as French outposts. Then pick one site to research more extensively.

French Place-names

_____   _____

_____   _____

_____   _____

_____   _____

_____   _____

_____   _____

_____   _____

_____   _____

_____   _____

(continued)

Name ______________________________

Date ______________________________

UNIT 4 **WORKSHEET 1**
Indian Cultures of the Great Lakes Region Meet the French Voyageurs

French Influence in the Heartland *(continued)*

Site selected: ______________________________

Date first settled: ______________________________

Origin of name: ______________________________

Why the French chose this location: ______________________________

What was this settlement used for? ______________________________

____

____

How was the settlement governed? ______________________________

____

____

____

Approximate population during French control? ______________________________

When and how did this site become part of either the British colonial empire or the United States?

____

____

____

____

Any current examples of French influence (architecture, shops, food, families of French descent)?

____

____

____

____

© 1997 J. Weston Walch, Publisher

Cultural Exchanges

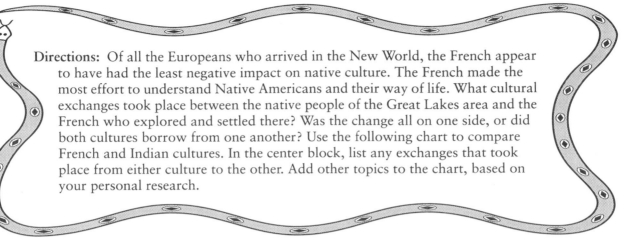

Directions: Of all the Europeans who arrived in the New World, the French appear to have had the least negative impact on native culture. The French made the most effort to understand Native Americans and their way of life. What cultural exchanges took place between the native people of the Great Lakes area and the French who explored and settled there? Was the change all on one side, or did both cultures borrow from one another? Use the following chart to compare French and Indian cultures. In the center block, list any exchanges that took place from either culture to the other. Add other topics to the chart, based on your personal research.

	Native American	Exchange	French
Religious beliefs			
Food			
Clothing			
Transportation			
Housing			

A Page from the Past

Native American Boats

When most people think of Native American watercraft, they usually think of Huron birchbark canoes skimming along the rivers and lakes of the Northeast. Native Americans built many different kinds of boats, however. The Beothuk built sturdy canoes made of elm bark. These boats were higher in the middle, bow, and stern to withstand the rough Atlantic Ocean. From the Penobscots in Maine down the coast to Florida, Native American tribes made dugout canoes. They used a large single tree for each boat. They hollowed out the tree by burning and gouging out the interior with stone scraping tools. These dugouts were sturdy oceangoing craft used for fishing and traveling to outer islands, such as Nantucket, off Massachusetts, and the Sea Islands, off Georgia and South Carolina.

In the interior, along the Missouri River, tribes such as the Mandan constructed bull boats. These round boats had rush frames covered with buffalo skins. They were used to cross rivers. Because of their shape, they were often at the mercy of the current and took great skill to steer.

In the Pacific Northwest, the Haida and Kwakiutl tribes made large oceangoing canoes out of huge cedar logs. These canoes could carry up to 70 people. They were used to hunt whale and other sea mammals. Tribe members often traveled hundreds of miles in these canoes on trading expeditions.

In the treeless Arctic, the Inuit used sealskin stretched over a bone or antler frame to construct the one-man hunting kayak. Tightened drawstrings on a waterproof shield enabled these craft to turn over and be righted without filling with water. This was the origin of the "eskimo roll" that every kayaker has to master. The Inuit also built umiaks. These were skin-covered craft used to transport entire families and their belongings over long distances.

Europeans in North America were impressed with the seaworthiness of Native American boats. French voyageurs adopted the canoes of the Hurons, which they found much safer and swifter than the Europeans' wide-keeled skiffs. Scientists are currently investigating the possibilities that Native Americans traveled great distances in their boats, perhaps even crossing the Atlantic to Europe.

5. Indian Cultures of the Northeast Meet the British Colonists

Beading designs made from birchbark

Indian Cultures of the Northeast Meet the British Colonists

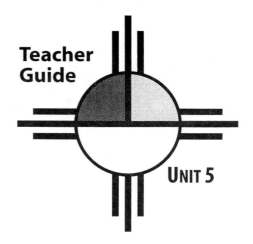

The northeastern region of the United States has many places with names of Indian origin—Massachusetts, Ossipee, Pemaquid, Pawtucket, and the lake with probably one of the longest names in the world, Lake Chargo- ggagoggmanchaugagoggchaubunagungamaug.*
 Unfortunately, names are sometimes all that remains of the once populous Native American tribes of New England. Many tribes are now extinct. How did this happen, and why in New England?

The Northeast coast of the United States was where Europeans—primarily British colo- nists—first settled in large numbers. Unlike those from other European nations, most British colonists came to stay. Most came as part of a family unit. They were not seasonal fisherman or trappers and fur traders who took what they could from the land with no notion of acquiring territory. English settlers often sought a new country for religious or political reasons. They wanted to obtain land and establish permanent settlements.

This unit introduces the consequences of contact between Native American tribes of the Northeast and English settlers. The story of the Pilgrims is no doubt familiar to many students. The Student Information Sheet focuses on the period before the Pilgrims landed and then on the aftermath of these early contacts between the Indians and settlers.

Preparation for This Unit

A good starting point might be the Indian place-names in New England or in the area where you live. What evidence is there of the Native American tribes that once inhabited your region? Are there any reservations, Indian terri- tories, or nations nearby?

Since diseases were so significant in the decline of the Indian populations of the North- east, you might wish to explain a *virgin soil epidemic*, which occurs when disease microbes are brought to a place where they have never been, where there are no natural immunities, so that even routine illnesses like chicken pox can be deadly.

Student Activities

Worksheet 1 is a list of research topics for student essays. We have suggested a length for the essay, but you may set your own standards. Worksheet 2 asks students to examine what might motivate the British colonists of different social status and occupations to settle in the New World. Although immigrants came to North America from all over Europe after 1800, initial settlement along the East Coast was, for the most part, people from the British Isles.

---

* The translation is something like "You fish on your side, I'll fish on mine, and all will fish in the middle."

Indian Cultures of the Northeast Meet the British Colonists

Arrival of Henry Hudson in the Bay of New York, September 2, 1609

When the **Puritans** first landed in New England, they were appalled by the disease and death that surrounded them. Skulls and bone fragments told of a plague that had destroyed much of the area's Native American population. The Puritans, meanwhile, felt that the devastation was God's will. That would make it easier for them to take control of the land without having to overcome any human obstacle. Disease, enslavement, and finally open warfare came out of the meeting between European and native cultures in the Northeast. The result was that the Native Amerindian population of southern New England was almost totally destroyed.

Indian Culture Before the Europeans Arrived

Before the Europeans arrived, Native Americans in the northeastern part of the United States lived in small villages. The villages were ruled by a chief, or *sachem*. They were usually independent, held together by strong matrilineal ties. Sometimes the sachem was a woman. This was a distinct cultural difference between Native Americans and colonists arriving from Europe, where women rarely aspired to any position of leadership.

Northeast Amerindian families lived in round wigwams or rectangular longhouses. Both of these dwellings were constructed of bent wood frames covered with bark or mats of woven plant material. They survived by fishing, hunting, and farming. Agriculture was practiced less in northern New England because the growing season was short. Native American farmers cultivated corn, beans, squash, pumpkins, Jerusalem artichokes, and other crops. Entire village groups sometimes traveled during the year, following a route determined by seasonal food staples. In the spring and summer, they moved

(continued)

Native Americans:
A Thematic Unit on Converging Cultures

Indian Cultures of the Northeast Meet the British Colonists *(continued)*

to tidal areas. There they harvested shellfish. They also moved to areas where there were berries and fruits to pick. In the winter, they moved into the forests. There they hunted a variety of animals and birds, including bear, deer, turkey, and waterfowl.

Warfare between tribal groups was common. European settlers later used this to their advantage. They pitted one tribe against another to weaken Native American resistance to the newcomers. Despite constant warfare, tribes often traded among themselves. They exchanged items such as beads, porcupine quills, furs, wooden bowls, and shells. The Pequot tribe were particularly famous traders of *wampum*. Wampum were highly valued beads made from purple or white shells.

Explorers and Settlers Come to the Land

There was a long history of contact between Europeans and the tribes of the Northeast. Some scholars believe that the Vikings visited this area. But conclusive evidence has never been found. In 1497, an Italian from Genoa, Italy, Columbus's hometown, sailed from England, in search of a trade route to the East. The seaman, Giovanni Caboto, is known to us as John Cabot. With financial backing from King Henry VII, he came upon a forested land, which he claimed for England and named Newfoundland. He publicized his voyage and emphasized the rich fishing areas, now known as the Grand Banks.

Fishermen from Europe probably fished the Grand Banks before Cabot's voyage. But they kept the location secret to thwart competition. News of Cabot's voyage spread rapidly. Ships from England, Portugal, and France crossed the Atlantic to take advantage of the fishing resources. Fishing was an important industry in Europe at the time. Most of Europe was Roman Catholic; Catholics ate no meat on Fridays and other fast days. Fish could also be dried and preserved for transport. Throughout the sixteenth century, fishermen from Europe landed on the north coast of North America. They set up temporary settlements, mended their nets, dried their fish, and then returned home. These fishermen also made the first contact with Native Americans on the coast. They began to trade European goods, such as cloth, metal ornaments, and glass beads, for furs and hides. Fur traders followed the fisherman from Europe and moved farther inland.

Conflict broke out almost immediately. European settlers often mistreated Indian women. They kidnapped natives for slaves. Most disastrous of all, they brought European illnesses, against which Native Americans had no immunity. Between 1616 and 1617, more than a third of New England's 25,000 Native Americans died in an epidemic. Historians are not certain which disease caused such a plague. It may have even been a common childhood illness, such as measles or chicken pox.

Europeans often captured Indians as slaves. In 1614, an English sea captain kidnapped 24 Indians from the New England coast and sold them as slaves in Spain. One of them, Tisquantum, or Squanto, escaped and made his way to England. In 1619, he came back to New England. in 1620, he astounded the Pilgrims at Plymouth when he greeted them in English. He was invaluable in helping the Plymouth colony survive. He acted as a translator. He taught the Pilgrims how to plant corn.

These first permanent settlers depended on the Indians to share knowledge of the land and

(continued)

Native Americans:
A Thematic Unit on Converging Cultures

Indian Cultures of the Northeast Meet the British Colonists
(continued)

Wampanoag chief Metacom, known as King Philip

teach them how to survive. More settlers followed. They brought the latest European technology to add to the settlers' newfound knowledge. Gradually, the colonists became more self-reliant. They began to regard the Native Americans as obstacles to obtaining land. Hostilities between settlers and native peoples increased. Atrocities occurred on both sides. The Europeans set Indian against Indian, profiting from intertribal rivalries. For example, in 1637, an army of 90 Englishmen, along with Indian allies mostly from the Narragansett tribe, marched on a Pequot village. Some 500 Pequots were killed. Following the battle, more Pequots were shipped off to Bermuda and the West Indies as slaves.

By 1662, **English** settlers in New England numbered 40,000—twice as many as Native Americans. The settlers overran traditional hunting grounds. They forced their religious beliefs on the native peoples. They refused to recognize the **sovereignty** of the tribes. Indians often entered into land deals without really understanding the terms. Land ownership was a foreign concept to most of them. So, they signed away their rights to traditional uses of the land. The chief of the Wampanoag tribe from 1661 to 1676 was Metacom. He was known to the English as "King Philip." Metacom was disgusted with the way the English treated the Indians. He began uniting the tribes of the region into a confederation to resist European violation of Indian lands. In 1675, hostilities turned into a full-scale war. The conflict was known as King Philip's War.

The war was over by the summer of 1676. Metacom and his followers were killed. The conflict was devastating to both Indians and colonists. The English lost 600 lives and over 1,200 homes. The war almost totally destroyed

(continued)

Native Americans:
A Thematic Unit on Converging Cultures

© 1997 J. Weston Walch, Publisher

Indian Cultures of the Northeast Meet the British Colonists *(continued)*

the Indian tribes of southern New England. More than 3,000 Indians were killed. Hundreds of others were enslaved and shipped to Virginia, the Caribbean, Spain, Portugal, and North Africa. Some of the smaller tribes were totally eliminated. The larger Wampanoag and Narragansett tribes were reduced to a few hundred people.

Aftermath

King Philip's War marked the end of Indian power in New England. Elsewhere in the Northeast, powerful tribes like the Iroquois Confederation continued to interact with the settlers. These tribes often used the rivalry between the English and French to their advantage. By the time of the American Revolution, however, Native American power in the Northeast was negligible. Native lands were overrun by colonists.

Today, some of the Northeast Indian tribes are making a comeback. The Mashantucket Pequots of Connecticut have built a casino and resort that makes a large profit for the tribe. Some of that money has been used to build a tribal museum and hire scholars to research the tribe's history. Many tribes have created educational programs and websites to share their

heritage. Plimoth Plantation, a Massachusetts "living" museum, includes a re-created Wampanoag village alongside the Pilgrims. But it is important to remember that other tribes, like the Nipmucks, are gone forever.

Glossary of Terms for This Unit

English: England is only one part of the island of Great Britain. Wales, although separate in language and culture, became part of England in the 1530's. Scotland was an independent country until 1707. Inhabitants of England are referred to as English. But colonists in America could be Welsh or Scottish as well. Collectively, all three groups are referred to as British.

matrilineal: A culture that traces the line of descent through women.

Puritans: A Protestant group in sixteenth- and seventeenth-century England who opposed certain formal practices within the Church of England and wished to "purify" it.

sovereignty: Independence, having the right to govern without any outside influence or control.

Name _____

Date _____

Research Paper

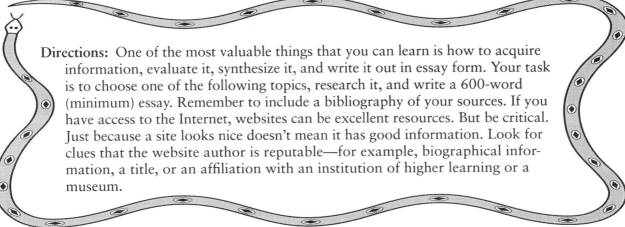

Directions: One of the most valuable things that you can learn is how to acquire information, evaluate it, synthesize it, and write it out in essay form. Your task is to choose one of the following topics, research it, and write a 600-word (minimum) essay. Remember to include a bibliography of your sources. If you have access to the Internet, websites can be excellent resources. But be critical. Just because a site looks nice doesn't mean it has good information. Look for clues that the website author is reputable—for example, biographical information, a title, or an affiliation with an institution of higher learning or a museum.

Topics	
Squanto	The real Pocohontas
The lost colony of Roanoke	Indian place-names and their meanings
The voyages of Henry Hudson	The "red paint people"
The French and Indian Wars	The Pequot War
King Philip's War	Roger Williams and his relations with Indians
The Mayflower Compact	Native American agriculture
The Pilgrims	The founding of Connecticut Colony
The Puritans and the founding of Boston	

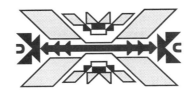

© 1997 J. Weston Walch, Publisher

Native Americans:
A Thematic Unit on Converging Cultures

Who Came Here, and Why?

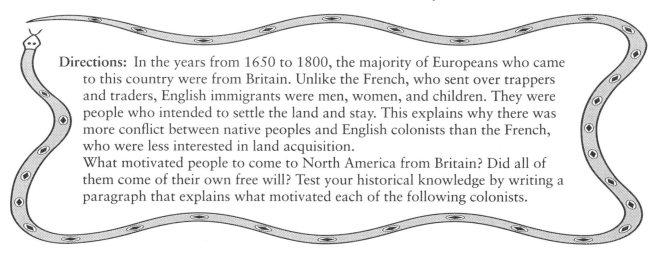

Directions: In the years from 1650 to 1800, the majority of Europeans who came to this country were from Britain. Unlike the French, who sent over trappers and traders, English immigrants were men, women, and children. They were people who intended to settle the land and stay. This explains why there was more conflict between native peoples and English colonists than the French, who were less interested in land acquisition.

What motivated people to come to North America from Britain? Did all of them come of their own free will? Test your historical knowledge by writing a paragraph that explains what motivated each of the following colonists.

Colonist	Possible motives for immigration
Farmer from County Essex	
Debtor from London	
Puritan from St. Botolph's town	
Highlander from Scotland	
Convicted felon from Bristol	
Craftsman from a rural village	
An indentured servant	

© 1997 J. Weston Walch, Publisher
Native Americans:
A Thematic Unit on Converging Cultures

A Page from the Past

Location, Location, Location! New York City

From the beginning, the area that is now New York City was a valuable and desirable location. Originally, Manhattan Island was populated by Native Americans of the Algonquian language group. Good fishing, where the Hudson River flowed into the Atlantic Ocean, drew them to the island. Hundreds of years of Native American life and culture changed dramatically after the European explorers arrived.

According to written records, the first European to explore the site of New York City was Giovanni da Verrazano. Verrazano was an Italian sailing in the service of the King of France. He sailed around the island of Manhattan in 1524. Afterward, he wrote that it was a land of beauty which seemed to have some value. For 85 years, no one followed up on Verrazano's discovery. In 1609, Englishman Henry Hudson landed on Manhattan Island. Hudson was employed by the Dutch East India Company. He was looking for a Northwest Passage to India, which, of course, he did not find. He sailed upriver about 150 miles. He went as far as present-day Albany and charted the course of what later was named the Hudson River.

In 1624, a few Dutch families settled in the area of Manhattan Island. In 1626, the Dutch West India Company sent Peter Minuit, a German from the Rhineland, to be director general of the Dutch colony of New Netherlands. Some history books say that Minuit made one of the greatest deals in the history of real estate. They say that he bought the island of Manhattan from the Indians for 60 guilders' (about $24) worth of trinkets. Other historians believe that Minuit gave goods to the Canarsee tribe for the *use* of Manhattan. The Canarsee tribe lived across the East River in what is today Brooklyn—not on Manhattan Island. Thus, the question is whether they had authority to make agreements about the island. The Weckquaesgeeks, who lived on the upper part of Manhattan, eventually demanded payment for Dutch use of the island. The popularity of the "$24 in trinkets" story reflects European feelings about how easy it was to dupe Native Americans.

In 1653, the Dutch settlement of New Amsterdam became a city. It had a population of 800 Europeans. Because of its good harbor, New Amsterdam was a center for trade between Europeans and Native Americans. The Dutch strengthened their position on Manhattan by winning several battles with local tribes. Dutch control ended in 1664 when an English fleet seized the city. New Amsterdam was renamed New York, after the Duke of York, brother of Charles II of England. By the end of the American Revolution, New York was the largest city in the new United States. It has remained the nation's largest city. In the latest census, its population stood at 7,322,564.

In European exploration and settlement, as in real estate today, location was everything. New York's position at the mouth of the Hudson River and its protected deepwater harbor have made it a location of power and prestige the world over. There is an interesting historical footnote. After Minuit left the Dutch West India Company, he went to work for the New Sweden Company. In 1638, he led settlers into what is now Delaware to establish a Swedish colony. The group settled on land he "purchased" from the native peoples of that area. Multinational competition for land and profit is not something found only in recent history.

Name _____

Date _____

A Page from the Past

The Hodenosaunee (Iroquois) Confederation

A common misconception exists about native peoples of North America. It holds that they were unable to organize into groups larger than tribes or collections of clans. In reality, there were several confederations of tribes. Probably the greatest of these was the Iroquois Confederation, centered in modern-day New York State. "Iroquois" was what Europeans called these formidable warriors of the Northeast. The Iroquois called themselves Hodenosaunee. That name meant "people of the long-houses." The tribes lived in long rectangular buildings that housed many families.

Before the confederation, the New York tribes lived in a state of feuding and warfare. According to legend, Onondaga chieftain Hiawatha became consumed with grief at the death of family members. He was comforted by a spiritual leader called Deganawida. Together, Hiawatha and Deganawida composed the laws of the "great league of peace," or "the great binding law." Then they persuaded the chiefs of five tribal nations,—the Mohawk, Oneida, Cayuga, Seneca, and Onondaga—to join in an alliance.

The exact date that the Five Nations joined together is not known. It is believed to be sometime in the sixteenth century, shortly before Europeans arrived. The laws of the great peace not only established accord among the nations but also set up a series of conventions to preserve the peace. Each of the Five Nations sent representatives to a grand council. The council was held yearly to resolve any disputes and reaffirm the alliance. Ceremonies at the council symbolized the bond of confederation. For example, five arrows were bound together to illustrate words from the great binding law: "As the five arrows are strongly bound, this shall symbolize the complete union of the nations. Thus are the Five

Nations united completely and enfolded together, united into one head, one body, and one mind. Therefore they shall labor, legislate, and council together for the interest of future generations."*

The League of the Hodenosaunee became the Six Nations when the Tuscarora joined in 1722. The league kept peace among its members but not between the Six Nations and outside tribes. Some historians see the Iroquois Confederation as the first formal union of people in America. Benjamin Franklin referred to the league when he proposed a union of the American colonies at the Albany Congress, in 1754.

The American Revolution ultimately split the League of the Six Nations. Some tribes chose to fight for the British. Some fought for the colonists.

People of Iroquois ancestry are often scattered far from their original homelands today. Yet, there is still a sense of solidarity, as evidenced by Mohawk ironworkers. These skilled laborers have worked on most of the skyscrapers in major North American cities. They are famous for their ability to work fearlessly high above the ground. From building alliances to building skyscrapers, descendants of the Hodenosaunee League remain an important part of our society.

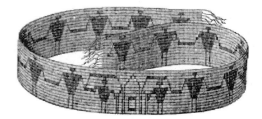

Wampum belt that may have represented the founding of the Iroquoian Confederation

_____

* From the Constitution of the Iroquois Nations: The Great Binding Law, Gayanashagowa

© 1997 J. Weston Walch, Publisher

54

*Native Americans:
A Thematic Unit on Converging Cultures*

6. The Indian Cultures of the Pacific Northwest

Hat (top) and masks from Northwest tribes

The Indian Cultures of the Pacific Northwest: Adapting to Fur Traders and Entrepreneurs

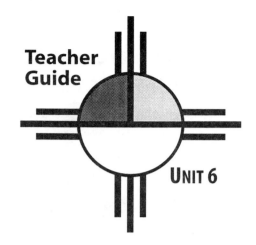

Teacher Guide

Unit 6

The story of tribes on the Northwest coast is different from that of tribes on the Northeast coast of North America. In both cases, diseases brought by the explorers and settlers took their toll. This is a recurring tragedy in the history of cultures in convergence. Native Americans of the Pacific Northwest, though, seemed better able to withstand European dominance. The earliest Europeans to arrive in the Northwest were not settlers anxious for land and homesteads. They were traders. Native Americans, used to trade among tribes, assumed an active role. The Europeans often relied totally on Native Americans' trading skills.

The artistic and cultural life of the Northwest helped preserve the tribes' identity. A strong sense of history, ceremony, and art gave Northwest cultures strength and permanence. In the late nineteenth and early twentieth centuries, anthropologists studied Northwest Amerindians intensively. They carefully described their way of life and culture. Northwest Native Americans today have not only rich oral traditions to keep their culture alive but also extensive written and film documentation.

Preparation for This Unit

This unit lends itself to discussing the importance of keeping history and tradition alive. How would you record or remember your history if, like most Native Americans, you had no written language? How do customs, ceremonies, traditions, and storytelling preserve a people's history and identity? You might ask students if they have any family customs—for example, a certain special way that birthdays are celebrated—that are passed down from generation to generation.

Student Activities

Worksheet 1 asks students to design a totem pole like those that Northwest tribes created. Students must decide what symbols best represent either themselves or their family. The second activity centers on storytelling, an important part of Native American culture. Students begin by studying a myth or legend from Northwest Indian culture. Then they write an original legend or myth to explain a natural phenomenon (a rainbow, the wind, the seasons), their family history, or an important event in their community or cultural heritage.

Indian Cultures of the Pacific Northwest:
Adapting to Fur Traders and Entrepreneurs

Tsimshian skin apron with painted decoration
and quilled embroidery

Imagine going to a ceremonial gathering that had been in preparation for 12 years. As a guest, you would receive gifts and be lavishly fed and entertained. This event, known as a potlatch, was one of the most important cultural traditions of the Northwest coast Indians. Perhaps more than any other Native American group, Northwest tribes are known for ceremonial rituals, dances, and artwork.

Anthropologists believe that the physical environment contributed to the kind of life the Northwest tribes developed. The culture included advanced rituals and high artistic achievement. The Pacific Northwest climate was mild compared with that of other areas of the West. Only the Canadian-Alaskan border areas experienced heavy snow and freezing weather. Materials for food and shelter were abundant. Shellfish, sea mammals, and salmon provided a stable food source. A small fish called a eulachon, or candlefish, yielded a nutritious oil. The forests supplied building materials for homes and huge seagoing canoes. These conditions meant the Northwest tribes had

more permanent settlements than some other cultures.

During the summer, tribes acquired enough food for the whole year. In the winter, they held ceremonies honoring the spirits of their ancestors and celebrating the natural bounties of their environment. They also created works of art in a distinctive style that is internationally recognized and prized by collectors.

Indian Culture Before the Arrival of the Europeans

Because food was plentiful, Native American populations were dense on the Northwest coast. As many as 46,000 Indians lived on the coast of British Columbia as late as 1835. Northwest tribes, like most Native Americans, were remarkably diverse in language and culture. But they also had certain features in common. They lived in village communities, usually close to the ocean or rivers. These villages were permanent communities, inhabited for hundreds of years.

(continued)

Indian Cultures of the Pacific Northwest: Adapting to Fur Traders and Entrepreneurs

(continued)

The village populations ranged from 50 to several hundred people. Each dwelling usually housed an extended family.

Houses were built of wooden planks, usually red cedar. Building a house was often an elaborate process marked by ceremonies and feasts. Houses were very large. They often had intricate carvings that used the family emblem, or crest—much as European nobility during the Middle Ages used **heraldic** symbols. There was a central hearth and an opening in the roof to let out the smoke. There were no windows. Sometimes there was a secret tunnel for use in ceremonies or as an escape route in case of attack. Doorways to the house often had a carved design of an animal figure, with the creature's open mouth as the entrance.

Among the Northwest people, family ties and **kinship** were of utmost importance. **Ancestry** determined many things. These included leadership roles in the village, use of resources in a certain geographic location, and dances or ceremonies that could be performed. Each clan, or group with shared descent, was represented by a crest—somewhat like a coat of arms. Crest designs usually represented spirits connected with a particular family. Some of the spirits included a bear, a whale, a human figure, or the sun. Crests expressed not only the importance of the clan but also each family's unique history. Spirits beneficial to the family's ancestors were depicted on canoes, blankets, storage boxes, and tools.

Fundamental to the Northwest tribes' understanding of kinship was the potlatch. Potlatch is a term meaning "to give." It came from a common trading language developed by the Chinook. Potlatches were intricate ceremo-

nies. They are difficult to explain due to their variety and complexity. They combined elements of political, social, religious, and economic life.

Basically, a potlatch was given to affirm a family privilege, such as the hereditary right to a title or a name. The host chief invited guests from other families and villages and gave them food and many gifts. Through dance, speeches, songs, and artwork, the host family related its history and emphasized its special birthright. By accepting the food and gifts, the guests were acting as witnesses and affirming the heritage of the host. Some potlatches were so huge that the host would have nothing left at the end, having given all material possessions away. This was unimportant. People believed that what the host lost in material goods he gained in honor and prestige. The potlatch served as a way to pass on the cultural heritage and to build up an oral tradition of tribal history.

The artwork of the Northwest tribes was closely allied to their ceremonies and kinship. Art was part of every aspect of daily life. Even the simplest objects were often ornately decorated with **curvilinear** designs. Three principal art forms were wood carving, painting, and weaving.

Northwest Indian food tray made from a hollowed-out block of wood

(continued)

Indian Cultures of the Pacific Northwest:
Adapting to Fur Traders and Entrepreneurs
(continued)

Trade was an important activity all along the Northwest Coast. The Haida and Kwakiutl tribes built large canoes that were seaworthy on the open ocean. Tribes from the Northwest may have traveled as far south as the coast of California.

Explorers and Settlers Come to the Land

When the first Europeans came to the Northwest coast, native peoples there began an active trade with the newcomers. As a result, they gained some useful new products. For example, with European iron blades they carved ornate totem poles.

The first report from from a European exploring the Northwest coast came from Apostolos Valerianos. He was a Greek sailing for Spain from 1588 to 1594 under the name Juan de Fuca. He claimed to have crossed a large inlet and reached countries with riches of gold. This account, although false, encouraged further exploration of the area. Always there was hope of discovering a passage connecting the Atlantic and Pacific Oceans.

In 1741, Russian explorer Alexey Chirikov landed in the southern part of Alaska. His reports encouraged the Russians to pursue a claim to the area. The Russians were not interested in settlement but in trade—particularly in furs.

Fearing that the Russians might be moving toward California, the Spanish acted. They sent Juan Perez to claim the Northwest coast for Spain in 1774. Perez never went ashore. However, he traded with about 200 Haida who

came out in canoes to meet the Spanish ships. The Haida **bartered** furs and handwoven blankets in return for cloth, beads, and metal knives.

The Spanish never seriously followed up their claim to the Northwest. The British, however, pursued trade with the Native Americans there. English explorer James Cook, in 1778, landed close to the present-day city of Vancouver. Cook obtained in trade many sea otter furs. He sold them in China at an enormous profit. Ships from Britain and the United States were soon sailing along the coast to trade for sea otter and other goods. The Northwest tribes participated actively in this trade. They used the goods they obtained to enrich their ceremonial and artistic life. The Chinook, in particular, dominated trade with Europeans. They already had a long-standing role as middlemen in intertribal trade. Chinook **jargon** became the common trading language for Indians and Europeans. For example, the trade jargon for any trader from the United States was a "Boston." That was because so many merchant ships came from Boston.

Huge land-based trading companies replaced merchant ships in the early 1800's. Some tribes opposed building trading posts and forts. Most, however, accepted the companies as a way to boost their trade and profits. The Hudson's Bay Company dominated the Northwest fur trade. This solidified Britain's claim to the territory. The European traders were not interested in settling the Indian lands. Therefore, conflicts were not as serious as in other North American areas. The worst threat to the Northwest tribes was the disease that the Europeans brought.

(continued)

Indian Cultures of the Pacific Northwest:
Adapting to Fur Traders and Entrepreneurs
(continued)

Aftermath

By the mid-nineteenth century, the fur trade had lost its importance. The Northwest began to be a destination for white settlers eager for land. The coastal region was split by treaty between the United States and Britain. This meant some tribes were also split. They ended up under the jurisdiction of two different nations. When Russia sold Alaska to the United States, the Tlingits protested. They claimed that the $7.2 million purchase price should have been paid to them, since the land belonged to their tribe.

All in all, Northwest tribes seem to have been the most successful at keeping their culture, lifestyle, and, in some cases, their ancestral lands. Despite being banned by the Canadian government from 1885 to 1950 as wasteful, the potlatch is still practiced today. Other rituals and traditions also survived, giving Pacific Northwest tribes a continued sense of identity.

—— Glossary of Terms for This Unit ——

ancestry: Family lineage, the people from whom you are descended.

anthropologists: Scientists who study the origin and development of human cultural, physical, and behavioral traits.

bartered: Traded object for object without using currency.

curvilinear: Design characterized by rounded lines; having no sharp angles.

heraldic: Having to do with heraldry, the study of genealogies, particularly the use of coats of arms and their use in demonstrating rank.

jargon: The specialized language of a particular trade or profession.

kinship: Being related to others by having common ancestors.

© 1997 J. Weston Walch, Publisher

Native Americans:
A Thematic Unit on Converging Cultures

Name _____

Date _____

UNIT 6   **WORKSHEET 1**
Indian Cultures of the Pacific Northwest:
Adapting to Fur Traders and Entrepreneurs

Make a Totem Pole

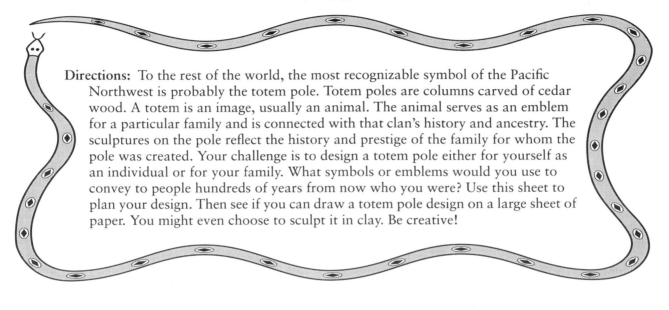

Directions: To the rest of the world, the most recognizable symbol of the Pacific Northwest is probably the totem pole. Totem poles are columns carved of cedar wood. A totem is an image, usually an animal. The animal serves as an emblem for a particular family and is connected with that clan's history and ancestry. The sculptures on the pole reflect the history and prestige of the family for whom the pole was created. Your challenge is to design a totem pole either for yourself as an individual or for your family. What symbols or emblems would you use to convey to people hundreds of years from now who you were? Use this sheet to plan your design. Then see if you can draw a totem pole design on a large sheet of paper. You might even choose to sculpt it in clay. Be creative!

Symbols of my history:

_____

_____

_____

Symbols of where I live:

_____

_____

_____

Symbols of who I am (hobbies, talents, interests):

_____

_____

_____

Other ideas: _____

_____

_____

Name _____

Date _____

UNIT 6 · WORKSHEET 2
Indian Cultures of the Pacific Northwest:
Adapting to Fur Traders and Entrepreneurs

The Importance of Myth and Storytelling

Directions: Myth and storytelling are the most important ways that tribal history is kept alive and native culture is passed from one generation to another. For thousands of years, Amerindians had no written languages. Through oral tradition, they maintained a history and a sense of the past. Here is a traditional story from the Pacific Northwest. After reading the story, answer the questions based on your reading. As an extra challenge, write your own story or myth. Your myth could explain a natural phenomenon, such as the change of the seasons. Or you could create a myth. The myth might tell about your family history. It might be about an event or place in your community. Or it might describe something in your own cultural background.

A Myth from the Tsimshian People of the Pacific Northwest*

A long time ago, the Tsimshian hunters were the strongest and cleverest humans in the world. They were such good hunters that all the large animals feared for their survival. The large animals decided to have a meeting at Grizzly Bear's house. At the meeting, they decided to ask the Creator to help them by making it very cold and sending deep snow to make it difficult for the hunters.

All the large animals, including Bear, Moose, and Panther, decided to have the small animals and insects join with them in asking the Creator to make the earth cold, dark, and snowy. All of the animals, large and small, had a meeting. Grizzly Bear told them of the plan and asked the small animals for their support. Porcupine spoke up, saying that the cold and snow might be fine for the large animals who had thick fat and warm fur, but that the small animals did not have those things; they needed warm weather to be able to live and find food. The insects, Mouse, and Rabbit agreed with Porcupine that they could not live in perpetual winter.

All the animals thought about what they could do to solve the problem. They reached a compromise. They decided to divide the year into six months of warmth and six months of cold.

Together, the animals went to the Creator and asked him to do this. In his wisdom, the Creator divided the year into seasons so that the large animals would not be continuously hunted.

- How would this myth transmit tribal pride to future generations?
- What natural phenomenon does this myth attempt to explain?

* Adapted from many sources, including *American Indian Myths and Legends*, selected and edited by Richard Erdoes and Alfonso Ortiz (New York: Pantheon Books, 1984).

7. The Five Civilized Tribes and the New American Nation

Pottery designs from early eastern tribes

The Five Civilized Tribes and the New American Nation

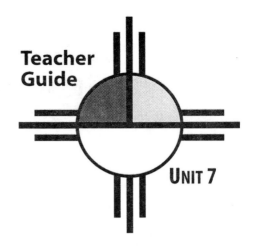
On May 26, 1838, the U.S. Army began rounding up the 17,000 members of the Cherokee nation. For 25 days, the army scoured the hills, fields, and valleys of the Cherokee homeland in Georgia, seized Cherokees as they worked on their farms or at their looms, and impounded them in stockades. The Cherokee, along with 80,000 other Native Americans from the Southeast, were forcibly deported to the newly designated Indian Territory west of the Mississippi River. The military commander, General Winfield Scott, wanted the operation to be carried out as humanely as possible. But brutality and terrible conditions still accompanied the forced deportation. To this day, the terrible 1,000-mile march westward is known as the Trail of Tears. It is commemorated by the Southeast tribes as a tragic event in their tribal history.

Their resilience and ability to adapt to the ways of settlers of European descent caused the Native Americans of the Southeast to become known as the Five Civilized Tribes. (It is interesting to note that they were called that because they adopted certain aspects of the white culture. The cultural bias of settlers of European descent made them equate anything that reflected their culture with "civilized" and anything that reflected Native American culture with "savage" or "primitive.") The Five Civilized Tribes—the Creeks, Chickasaws, Choctaws, Cherokees, and Seminoles—all suffered from white encroachment on their tribal lands. Most were forced to move to what is today Oklahoma. They continued to make progress in their new lands and soon brought a high level of civilization and culture to the prairie.

Preparation for This Unit

Many students seem to have a preconceived notion of how Native Americans should look and act—in the past and today. The Five Civilized Tribes really do not fit the stereotype: Indians living in tipis, wearing buckskins and bonnets of eagle feathers. By the end of the eighteenth century, the Cherokee were living either in log cabins or in plantation houses. They wove colorful cotton cloth. Many dressed exactly like non-Indians. It is important perhaps to touch on stereotypical views of Native Americans. As students read their Student Information Sheet, ask them to consider why the Indians were removed from their lands. What were the underlying motives for deporting them? All of the treaties that were signed stated that it was for their own good.

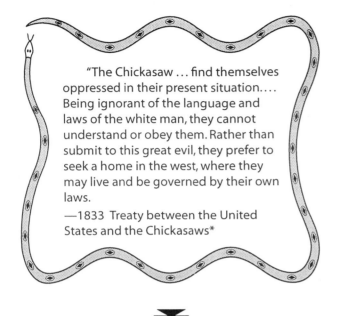

"The Chickasaw ... find themselves oppressed in their present situation.... Being ignorant of the language and laws of the white man, they cannot understand or obey them. Rather than submit to this great evil, they prefer to seek a home in the west, where they may live and be governed by their own laws.

—1833 Treaty between the United States and the Chickasaws*

Student Activities

The first activity is a good introduction to stereotypes and preconceptions. Students are asked to describe how they think of Native Americans with regard to such things as clothing and appearance, housing, and communication. They fill in this part of the activity sheet before they read the Student Information Sheet. After reading the Student Information Sheet, they are asked to describe the Cherokees around 1830, using the same framework. It might be interesting to provide students with pictures of some early Cherokee leaders, such as John Ross or Elias Boudinot.

The second activity is map work. Students are asked to trace the route from the original homeland of the Southeast tribes to the territory set aside for them in what became Oklahoma. What were the physical and environmental differences between the two areas? Was the land "exchange" a fair one?

*Jim Carnes, *Us and Them: A History of Intolerance in America* (Montgomery, AL: Southern Poverty Law Center, 1995), p.16.

The Five Civilized Tribes and the New American Nation

The Cherokee *Trail of Tears,* by Robert Lindneux

In the 1830's, more than 100,000 members of the Southeastern tribes were forced off their ancestral lands. They left Georgia, North and South Carolina, Tennessee, and Florida and walked 1,000 miles to the new Indian territory, in what is now Oklahoma. The Cherokee lost at least a quarter of their people during the trip west. They called the journey "the trail where we cried." Today, this coerced migration of the Southeastern tribes is known as the Trail of Tears.

The principal tribes of the Southeast were the Creek, Choctaw, Chickasaw, Seminole, and Cherokee. They had a long history of interaction with European newcomers. Many had reached the point of **acculturation** into European ways. For this reason, white settlers referred to them as the Five Civilized Tribes.

Indian Culture Before the Arrival of the Europeans

North American tribes of the Southeast differed a lot in language and culture. By the mid-eighteenth century, the Five Civilized Tribes predominated in the region. Smaller tribes died out, in many cases because of the diseases that Europeans brought. The Creeks were a confederacy of different languages and cultures. A large population and formidable warriors made the Creeks the dominant Indian nation of the Southeast.

All of the Amerindian groups were descended from the Mississippian culture. Huge Mississippian temple mounds are still visible in some areas. Despite their diversity of language, southeastern tribes all lived similarly. Most lived in towns, or chiefdoms, usually located near a

(continued)

The Five Civilized Tribes and the New American Nation *(continued)*

river or stream. Each town was built around a ceremonial center, or plaza. The plaza contained a townhouse for meetings, a summer council house, and a field for ceremonies and games. Family homes surrounded the plaza and public buildings. Families were grouped according to clan. Clans were defined as people related through the mother's line.

Family households often had several buildings: a winter house, a summer house, and storage buildings. The winter house was round with a floor dug into the ground. It was heavily insulated with clay and plant material, such as Spanish moss. The summer house was more open to allow for ventilation during the warm season. Saplings and reeds were interwoven with a framework of wooden posts topped by a gabled roof of pine bark.

Unlike the Mississippian culture, which had absolute rulers, the later native peoples of the Southeast had a more democratic government. The principal leader, or chief, was the executive officer of the town council. But his power was not unlimited. The town council was made up of all the men in the community. They met openly in a forum to discuss matters of daily importance.The town could send representatives to a council of the entire nation to deal with more serious issues, such as trade and war.

Explorers and Settlers Come to the Land

The Southeastern tribes and Europeans first met in 1513, when Juan Ponce de León landed in what is today Florida. Early contacts were not always peaceful. In 1521, two Spanish ships landed near the Savannah River. The Spanish enticed a number of Indians on board and captured them to sell as slaves. Hernando de

Soto's expedition through the Southeast in 1540 spread disease and destruction. The only early Europeans interested in settling in the area were a group of French Protestants, known as Huguenots. They tried to establish a settlement in Florida in 1564. Other Europeans were concerned with trade and building military forts to maintain their claim on the territory. The Spanish drove the Huguenots out in 1565.

A major turning point for the Southeast tribes came when British merchants founded Charles Town in 1670. These merchants were interested in two items: deerskins and Indian captives. They sold the captives as slaves for work in the West Indies, in New England, or on plantations in Carolina. Deer were hunted almost to extinction. In 1707, 121,000 deerskins were shipped to Europe. In search of more deer, tribes moved into territory where they did not traditionally hunt. The move caused intertribal rivalries and, ultimately, wars. Wars resulted in Indian captives, which helped supply the slave markets.

Throughout the seventeenth and eighteenth centuries, the British, French, and Spanish pitted tribes against one another to keep them weak and divided.

The Southeast tribes supported the British during the War of Independence. They feared that they would lose their territory to land-hungry Americans if the revolution succeeded. Indian wars continued in the Southeast through the early nineteenth century. Fighting raged between Indian groups as well as between American troops and native peoples. The largest Southeast tribes retained sizeable portions of their native lands. But pressure to obtain tribal lands for white settlement was building steadily.

The Five Civilized Tribes—Chicasaw, Choctaw, Seminole, Cherokee, and Creek—learned

(continued)

The Five Civilized Tribes and the New American Nation *(continued)*

early on to adopt certain aspects of European culture. Many Native Americans intermarried with white settlers. Some owned cotton plantations and black slaves. Tribes believed that assimilating into white culture and learning English would help them keep their ancestral lands. They invited missionaries to establish schools to teach English and various vocational skills. The Cherokee, in particular, were successful in assimilating the European culture. They built roads. They started schools. They owned sawmills. They produced woven cloth. And they established a constitution and court system. Sequoyah, a Cherokee warrior and scholar, spent years devising a system of writing for the Cherokee language. His alphabet of syllables was successful. Nearly the entire tribe became literate in a very short time. The *Cherokee Phoenix*, the tribe's own newspaper, began publication in 1828.

Sequoyah

Aftermath

Despite the **acculturation** of the "civilized" tribes, settlers still saw Indians as inferior and a block to their own ambitions. The year of decision was 1829. Andrew Jackson became president. Gold was discovered on Cherokee lands in Georgia. Many of the Southeast tribes had fought *with* Jackson in the War of 1812. But Jackson urged Congress to disown all earlier treaties with the Southeast tribes and pass his Indian Removal Act. Jackson felt that Native Americans should be removed to land west of the Mississippi for their own good. Some legislatures argued that it was criminal to overturn previous treaties. But the Removal Act passed by five votes.

Through bribes, double-dealing, and coercion, the Southeast tribes were pushed out. They were forced from their homelands and moved to the new Indian Territory, now Oklahoma. The Choctaws were the first to be moved. Of the 13,000 who left Mississippi and Alabama, over 4,000 died on the trip west. The Creeks and the Chickasaws were next. The Florida Seminoles proved to be the most difficult to remove. From 1835 to 1842, the U.S. government had to fight the Seminoles. It was one of the longest and costliest Indian wars in history. Some 4,000 Seminoles were eventually sent west. Some remained hidden in the Everglades. About 1,000 of their descendants live in Florida today. Escaped black and Indian slaves often found refuge with the Seminoles. There, they were accepted as part of the tribe.

The Cherokee fought removal by the wisest means. They took their case to the U.S. Supreme Court. The court ruled that the state of Georgia had no right to take the land. The ruling said that the Cherokee had the right to

(continued)

The Five Civilized Tribes and the New American Nation *(continued)*

self-government and independence. President Jackson, the state of Georgia, and federal officials ignored the court's decision. In 1833, Georgia held a lottery to sell Cherokee lands. Included in the sale were the capital, New Echota, and the plantations of many Cherokee leaders. The Cherokee leadership split into two factions. One side firmly opposed removal. The other side saw removal as the only alternative to bloodshed. While John Ross, the principal chief of the Cherokee, was pleading the tribe's case in Washington, a group of leaders signed a treaty. The treaty gave all of the tribe's lands east of the Mississippi to the U.S. government for $5 million. More than 80 percent of the tribe disavowed the treaty. But Jackson declared that the Cherokee nation no longer existed. He began preparations for the tribe's removal.

In 1838, 7,000 U.S. soldiers under the command of General Winfield Scott rounded up the 17,000 tribe members. For the 1,000-mile trip west, the Cherokee were allowed to take only what they could carry. As soon as they had left their homes, white settlers moved in to take over the land and any possessions left behind.

Chief Ross organized his people for the trek west. But the six-month journey in the fall and winter of 1838 to 1839 was marked by hardship, disease, and death. About 4,000 Cherokee died on the way.

At the end of the Trail of Tears was an unsettled prairie. The prairie was very different from these people's native lands to the east. The Five Tribes adapted to their new environment. They rebuilt the society and community that they had left behind. They constructed schools and churches. They established a tribal government. In 1907, the territory that had been given to the Southeast Indians became part of the new state of Oklahoma. Once again, settlers were allowed to claim large areas that Native Americans had been promised would remain theirs forever.

—— **Glossary of Terms for This Unit** ——

acculturation: Acquiring the culture (the way of life and customs) of another society.

John Ross

Test Your Bias

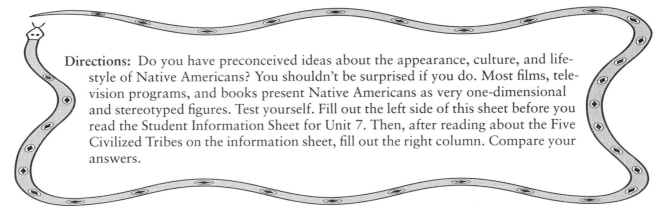

Directions: Do you have preconceived ideas about the appearance, culture, and life-style of Native Americans? You shouldn't be surprised if you do. Most films, television programs, and books present Native Americans as very one-dimensional and stereotyped figures. Test yourself. Fill out the left side of this sheet before you read the Student Information Sheet for Unit 7. Then, after reading about the Five Civilized Tribes on the information sheet, fill out the right column. Compare your answers.

	Your View of Native Americans	Cherokees in About 1830
Clothing and appearance		
Housing		
Methods of getting food		
Organization		
Communication		
Crafts and artwork		

The Trail Where We Cried: The Removal of Native Americans from the Southeast

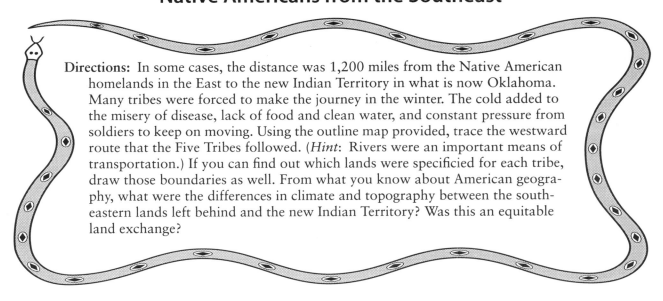

Directions: In some cases, the distance was 1,200 miles from the Native American homelands in the East to the new Indian Territory in what is now Oklahoma. Many tribes were forced to make the journey in the winter. The cold added to the misery of disease, lack of food and clean water, and constant pressure from soldiers to keep on moving. Using the outline map provided, trace the westward route that the Five Tribes followed. (*Hint*: Rivers were an important means of transportation.) If you can find out which lands were specificied for each tribe, draw those boundaries as well. From what you know about American geography, what were the differences in climate and topography between the southeastern lands left behind and the new Indian Territory? Was this an equitable land exchange?

Climate and Topography— Southeast	Climate and Topography— Indian Territory

(continued)

Name _____

Date _____

UNIT 7   **WORKSHEET 2**
**The Five Civilized Tribes and the New
American Nation**

The Trail Where We Cried:
The Removal of Native Americans from
the Southeast *(continued)*

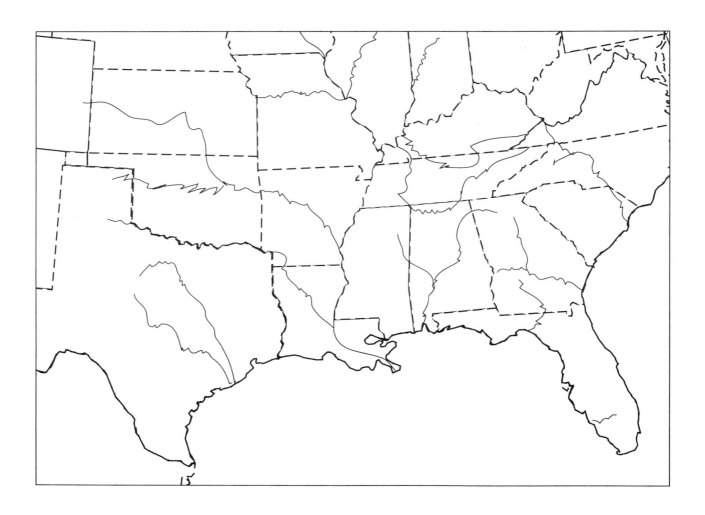

A Page from the Past

The Eastern Cherokee

Not all of the Cherokee people were forced to walk the Trail of Tears in 1838. Through luck, stealth, and personal sacrifice, about 1,000 Cherokees managed to remain in the East. They stayed in the mountains of western North Carolina. These Cherokee were known as the Eastern Band. Today, they make their homeland in Qualla Boundary, a reservation of 56,573 acres near Great Smoky Mountains National Park.

When soldiers came in 1838 to round up the Cherokees for removal to the West, some families escaped. They went into the thickly forested mountains, where there were no white settlements and where some small Cherokee bands already lived. According to Cherokee tradition, many resisted capture and helped others escape, as well. Tsali was one such hero.

Tsali killed a soldier who had brutalized his wife. He then fled with his family into the Smoky Mountains, where other Cherokee were hiding. General Winfield Scott and his soldiers pursued Tsali and other Indians through the mountains. But they were unsuccessful. In frustration, Scott declared that if Tsali gave himself up, the army would no longer pursue the Cherokees hiding in the mountains. Tsali surrendered. He was executed by firing squad. But Scott kept his promise. The Cherokee were left in their mountain home. Their descendants today make up the Eastern Band of the Cherokee.

Between 1843 and 1861, William H. Thomas, a lawyer and businessman who had grown up among the Cherokee, helped the Eastern Band. Thomas purchased land and held deeds for the tribe. (Initially, Cherokees were not legally permitted to own land, as individuals or as a tribe.) For 30 years, Thomas acted as an adviser to the tribe. Today, the land deeds are held in trust by the federal government. Only Cherokee can buy and sell land within the Qualla Boundary. The affairs of the tribe are governed by a chief, elected every four years, and a council, elected every two years. The tribal council controls public services—police and fire, schools, and economic development.

Cherokee, the principal town of Qualla Boundary, is a popular tourist attraction. It has a museum and a village that portray Cherokee life and crafts of the 1700's . Bingo is a big moneymaker for the tribe. The game is not restricted by state regulations because the reservation land is not legally part of North Carolina. Some tribe members earn a living by posing for photographs wearing warbonnets and standing next to tipis. Neither warbonnets nor tipis are part of the Cherokee culture. The Cherokees realize, however, that most visitors have a preconceived notion of how Indians should look, based on Hollywood Westerns. They are willing to bend the truth to make money for the tribe, whose main goal is economic self-sufficiency.

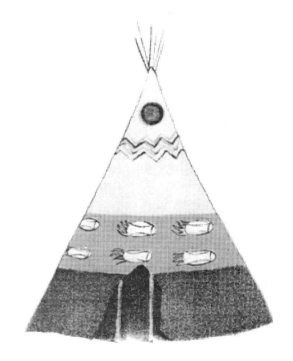

© 1997 J. Weston Walch, Publisher

Native Americans:
A Thematic Unit on Converging Cultures

8. The Indians of California

Acorns were an important crop for the California Indians.

The Indians of California: Diversity of Land and People

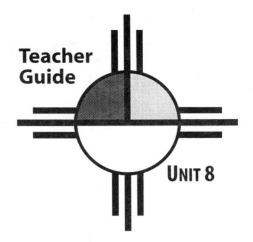

Teacher Guide

UNIT 8

The Gold Rush, Hollywood, Disneyland, Beverly Hills, the Golden Gate Bridge. California brings many images to mind. What may not spring to mind is the Native American population of the Golden State. The story of the California Indians is one of the saddest chapters in American history. What occurred in the nineteenth century was the near extinction of the state's native population.

In California, officials began to rethink the policy of removing tribes to new lands. Instead, they concentrated Indians within the state, in small reservations. The reservations were too small to support the native population. So, the Indians often became homeless wanderers, with no means of support. From an estimated 300,000 in the early 1700's, the Native American population of California fell to 17,000 by 1900. It currently stands at 236,078.

Preparation for This Unit

The treatment of the California Indians has often been labeled genocide. You may wish to discuss the meaning of this term with your students. There have been many genocides throughout history, the most disastrous being the annihilation of thousands of Jews by the Nazis. What other genocides have occurred?

Your students may wish to research the Armenian genocide, the "killing fields" in Cambodia, or the tragic events in East Africa during the 1990's. Can the destruction of the native peoples of California be called a genocide?

Student Activities

California is a land with great variation in climate and topography. Worksheet 1 asks students to look at the different geographic environments in California and evaluate them in terms of human habitation. For example, a river valley may provide fertile alluvial soil for cultivating crops, but there is always the danger of severe flooding, as occurred in Califoria in the winter of 1997.

Worksheet 2 examines why new settlers have always believed that California is a land of extraordinary opportunity. The state ranks first in population. Incredible ongoing growth probably sealed the fate of the native population in California more than anywhere else in the United States. A good follow-up activity might be to have students construct a time line of your state's history, evaluating factors that encouraged settlement and, therefore, displacement of the Native American population.

The Indians of California:
Diversity of Land and People

Indian woman gathering seeds

California has often been looked upon as America's golden land of opportunity. During the Great Depression, thousands of people from the dust-bowl states migrated to California in search of jobs. Today, most people associate California with the high-tech firms in Silicon Valley, Hollywood glamour, and TV shows like *Beverly Hills 90210*. As people have poured into California, making it the most heavily populated state in the nation, the state's early history has moved more and more into the background.

California was once the homeland of over 100 Native American tribes. What happened to

them, in the opinion of some scholars, is the closest thing to **genocide** that has ever occurred in this country. Compared with their numbers in the pre-European past, only a few Indians remain in California today. That any remain at all is testimony to their resilience and perseverance against adversity.

Indian Culture Before the Arrival of the Europeans

What was most remarkable about the Native Americans who lived in the California

(continued)

The Indians of California:
Diversity of Land and People *(continued)*

region, was their diversity. There were over 100 tribes. They spoke 90 distinct languages with 300 dialects. Unlike tribes on the East Coast, those on the West Coast avoided intertribal conflict. The land that the California Indians inhabited varied a great deal in geography and climate. Such variation contributed to the cultural diversity that evolved, as native people adapted to their environment.

The California Indians were not farmers. Instead, they hunted, fished, and gathered wild plants. They were so skillful at managing wild plants, it was as if they lived in an enormous wild garden. For example, they knew to burn certain areas to encourage beneficial plants to grow. They harvested bulbs, like the wild hyacinth. They kept some bulbs as food. And they divided and replanted the smaller bulbs to foster new growth. Tribes that lived near the coast gathered oysters, crabs, abalone, and mussels. Those who lived in the marshlands used tule, a plant like a cattail, for food and building material. They set out fish traps and hunted waterfowl. Acorns were a particularly important crop. The California Indians boiled out the acorn's bitter-tasting tannin. Then they used the nuts for bread, gruel, or soup.

Dwellings, as well as diet, reflected geography and climate. Indians in forested areas used cedar planks for houses. Those living in desert-like climates used lightweight materials, such as reeds, to allow air circulation. In cooler regions, people lived in pit houses, dug down into the earth.

There was some trade. But most California Indians stayed in one location. Seasonal migration to follow food supplies was less frequent than in other parts of North America. Native Americans used and managed resources in California in harmony with the environment. Early

European explorers and later settlers failed to understand this Indian attitude toward the natural world. They thought that California Indians were primitive and lazy compared with other Indian groups, like the Pueblo, who farmed. They made fun of the Indians. They called them "diggers" because they dug in the soil with pointed sticks. The newcomers had no idea that the Indians were actually caring for the land and harvesting plants, just as a skilled farmer would.

Explorers and Settlers Come to the Land

The first Europeans to explore California were the Spanish. They arrived in 1542. At that time, the Native American population of the region was probably 300,000. In 1769, a Franciscan friar named Father Junípero Serra, accompanied by Spanish soldiers, established a mission near what is today San Diego. This was the first of 21 Spanish missions, that reached north along the coast to the Bay of San Francisco. The reason for the military-missionary expeditions was twofold. First, they spread the Roman Catholic religion and Spanish culture among the native people. Second, they strengthened Spain's control over the territory it had claimed. The purpose of having a Spanish presence as far north as San Francisco was to block any Russian expansion down from Alaska.

Father Serra had hoped to attract Native Americans to the missions with the promise of food. But he found that native peoples were well sustained by the land. The Spaniards, however, had to barter for food themselves. They offered the Indians cloth and beads in exchange.

To convert native populations, Spanish missionaries followed a policy called *reduccíon*,

(continued)

Native Americans:
A Thematic Unit on Converging Cultures

The Indians of California:
Diversity of Land and People *(continued)*

or "concentration." Indians at each mission were isolated from their native customs and surroundings. By means of a "carrot" of enticement, such as glass beads, or a "stick" of military force, the Indians were brought under control. Once converted, the "neophytes," as they were called, were not allowed to leave the mission.

Mission Indians learned trades and how to herd and farm. They worked more like slaves than free laborers for the mission and its lands. Under the mission system, over 10,000 acres were brought into cultivation and thousands of horses and cattle were raised. The cattle industry became particularly important. Meat, hides, and tallow to supply the East were traded to ships that sailed around the Horn into California's coastal ports.

The treatment of Native Americans at the missions was often appallingly cruel. In 1799, a Franciscan friar wrote about the treatment. "For the slightest things, they receive heavy floggings, are shackled, and put in the stocks, and treated with so much cruelty that they are kept whole days without a drink of water."* In return for his observations, the friar was forced to leave California under armed guard.

Perhaps worse than the physical abuse was the disruption of the native economy. The cultivation of the land and the introduction of grazing animals upset the balance of nature. Horses and cattle stripped the land bare, leaving few wild plants for the Indians to harvest. Wild game was either driven away by the clearing of land or hunted indiscriminately by the Spanish. Native peoples, who once had abundant food, now depended on the mission for their meals and their livelihood. As with other native groups, diseases introduced by the newcomers took a terrible toll.

Mexico won independence and control of California from Spain in 1821. The missions then were **secularized,** and the neophytes were allowed to leave. With their traditional economy destroyed, most Indians had little choice but to stay at the missions. They became laborers for the Mexican ranchers who took over the mission lands. In 1848, the Mexican War ended. California changed hands again. It became part of the United States. Shortly afterward, gold was discovered in California. Then, Americans from the East and fortune hunters from around the world rushed to the territory.

Aftermath

The miners and other settlers overran native lands. Sometimes they killed Indians for sport. Other times they enslaved Indian children to work the gold diggings or farms. Although California was admitted to the union as a **free state,** government officials ignored the use of Indians as slaves. Between 1851 and 1900, the California Indian population decreased by 80 percent. By 1900, only 17,000 Indians were left in the state.

—— Glossary of Terms for This Unit ——

Franciscan friar: A member of an order of the Roman Catholic Church founded by St. Francis of Assisi, noted for missionary activities.

free state: A state where Negro slavery was prohibited before the Civil War.

genocide: The systematic destruction or annihilation of a racial, political, or cultural group.

secularized: Transferred from religious to nonreligious or civil control.

Geographic Diversity and Adaptation

Directions: What was most remarkable about the Native Americans of California was their ability to adapt to the varied geography in their state. Your task is to research the different geographic environments of California. What are the benefits for humans living in each environment? What challenges or difficulties does each environment present?

Environment	Benefit	Challenge
Marshland		
Desert		
Marine west coast climate		
Forested upland (Vertical)		
Temperate river valley		
Mediterranean climate		
Semiarid climate		

© 1997 J. Weston Walch, Publisher

Native Americans:
A Thematic Unit on Converging Cultures

Seeing the Elephant—Then and Now

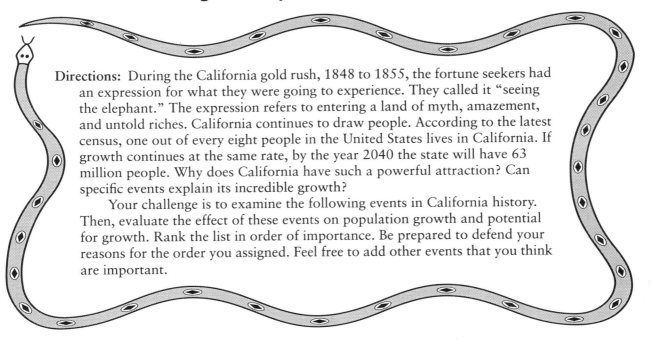

Directions: During the California gold rush, 1848 to 1855, the fortune seekers had an expression for what they were going to experience. They called it "seeing the elephant." The expression refers to entering a land of myth, amazement, and untold riches. California continues to draw people. According to the latest census, one out of every eight people in the United States lives in California. If growth continues at the same rate, by the year 2040 the state will have 63 million people. Why does California have such a powerful attraction? Can specific events explain its incredible growth?

Your challenge is to examine the following events in California history. Then, evaluate the effect of these events on population growth and potential for growth. Rank the list in order of importance. Be prepared to defend your reasons for the order you assigned. Feel free to add other events that you think are important.

Date	Event	Historical Significance	Rank
1542	Juan Rodgríguez Cabrillo sails from Mexico to explore the coast of California.		
1579	Sir Francis Drake lands on the coast near San Francisco Bay and claims California for Queen Elizabeth I of England.		
1602–1603	Sebastián Vizcaíno sails to find good ports and writes a favorable report about California.		
1769	Gaspar de Portolá and Father Junipero Serra arrive in California and establish the first mission.		
1826	"Mountain Man" Jedediah Smith travels to California.		
1840	First settlers cross the mountains and enter California from the east.		
1842	John Sutter buys Fort Ross from the Russians.		

(continued)

© 1997 J. Weston Walch, Publisher

Native Americans:
A Thematic Unit on Converging Cultures

Seeing the Elephant—Then and Now *(continued)*

Date	Event	Historical Significance	Rank
1845	Lansford W. Hastings publishes *The Emigrant's Guide to Oregon and California*.		
1846	The Donner party dies tragically.		
1848	The Treaty of Guadalupe Hidalgo ends the Mexican War.		
1848	Gold is discovered at Sutter's mill.		
1850	California becomes a state.		
1861	The Civil War begins.		
1869	Transcontinental railroad is completed.		
1870–1878	Drought hits California.		
1874	Southern Pacific Railroad is begun.		
1882	Chinese Exclusion Act is passed.		
1888	Refrigerated railroad cars carry produce across the country.		
1906	San Francisco earthquake strikes.		
1908	First Model T Ford is available to the public.		
1913	Los Angeles aqueduct is opened.		
early 1900's	Thomas Edison begins to pursue movie-makers who infringe on his patent.		
1929	The Great Depression begins.		
1935	Conditions in the Dust Bowl worsen.		
1943	Chinese Exclusion Act is repealed.		
1945	World War II ends and "baby boom" begins.		
1976	Steve Wozniak and Steve Jobs build the Apple I computer.		
1981	Microsoft reorganizes with Bill Gates as president.		
1989	San Francisco is rocked by a large earthquake.		

A Page from the Past

Ishi, The Last of His People

Imagine visiting a museum display that features artifacts from the culture of a *vanished* Indian tribe. Now, imagine finding out that part of the display includes an actual living tribe member. Ishi, the sole surviving member of the California Yahi Indians, spent the last five years of his life at the University of California's Museum of Anthropology. Ishi worked as a caretaker. He also worked with anthropologists to document his culture and language. And he demonstrated Yahi crafts to museum visitors. He even constructed a traditional summer shelter on the museum grounds.

Ishi's story typifies the tragic history of many California tribes destroyed by the influx of settlers seeking mineral riches or farmland. The Yana, a larger group to which the Yahi belonged, could not survive the newcomers' destruction of wild plants and game. Starving with hunger, they raided farms and ranches for food. Thousands of them were killed by white vigilantes. By 1872, only five Yahis were left alive. Ten-year-old Ishi was one of them.

In 1911, driven by hunger, Ishi came down from the mountains to the northern California town of Oroville. Newspapers carried stories about the "last wild Indian" being held in the Oroville jail. Alfred Louis Kroeber, an anthropologist at the University of California, suspected that this "wild Indian" might be a Yana. He sent a colleague to Oroville to converse with the man in simple Yana terms. Anthropologists confirmed that Ishi was, indeed, a Yana—the last living Yahi. Ishi never revealed his true name—a private matter in the Yahi culture. So, Kroeber called him Ishi, which means "one of the people."

At the Museum of Anthropology, Ishi met regularly with scientists. He helped them understand his culture and transcribe his language. He struggled to learn English. He adopted the clothing and manners of his hosts, as he felt a polite guest should do. He seemed to recognize his unique position and identity as a living remnant of the past.

Scientists traveled with Ishi to Yahi territory. They got to see Ishi in his own environment. For Ishi, it was a chance to be sure that the spirits of his ancestors were at rest. The Yahi believed that if the dead were not appropriately cremated, their spirits would wander. The first night, Ishi went into the woods alone. He returned at dawn, relieved that none of the spirits were lost. At the end of the trip, Ishi was content to return to the museum, which he now accepted as home.

Ishi died from tuberculosis in 1916. His hand-crafted objects, including a bow and a basket that held acorn meal, were cremated along with his remains. In the short time that Ishi lived in the modern world, he impressed everyone. He had an agreeable manner, a warmth, and a talent. He was the living legacy of a lost people.

9. The Plains Indians

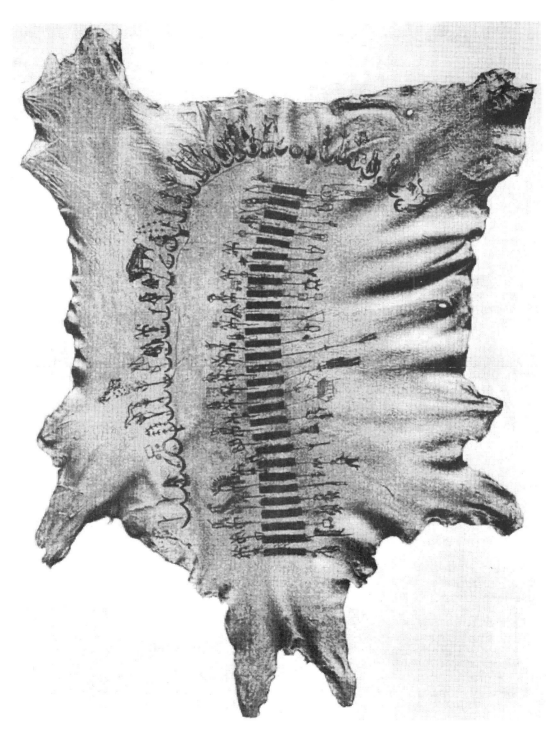

The Anko Calendar, a record of events of the Kiowa tribe

The Plains Indians: Cultures in Final Conflict

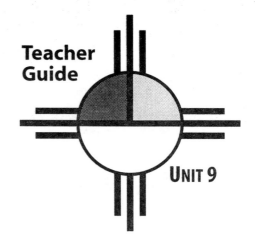

When most students think of Native Americans, they are picturing the Plains culture. The entertainment media have indelibly impressed on our minds the warbonneted chief and his followers on horseback. This cliché was popularized so successfully at home and abroad by Buffalo Bill Cody's Wild West Show that, during World War I, German soldiers especially feared an encounter with Native American U.S. soldiers because they still believed that the Indians carried tomahawks and scalped their enemies.

The final conflict for land between Native American and settler took place on the Plains at a time when newspapers, magazines, photography, and dime novels were extremely popular. The public was simultaneously fascinated and horrified to read of such events as Custer's Last Stand, which were reported in sensational graphic detail to stimulate sales. The fact that the conflict over Plains land coincided with the rise of popular journalism would be a good topic to discuss with your students.

Preparation for This Unit

Reviewing the American westward movement as well as the geography of the Great Plains is recommended. It is important that students understand why the Great Plains were at first bypassed by settlers. What forces eventually encouraged white settlers to come to the Great Plains, braving the challenging climate and limited resources, especially water?

Student Activities

The first activity asks students to put themselves in others' shoes to analyze the reasons for conflict over Plains territory, identifying different attitudes toward land acquisition and use. Worksheet 2 involves research on four great chiefs of the Plains tribes. Two worked for a peaceful resolution to the conflict over land, and two led their people in battle against the U.S. Army. What was the outcome for each of the four Native American leaders? Was either approach a success for the native people?

The Plains Indians:
Cultures in Final Conflict

Pictograph of the Battle of Little Bighorn

As settlers moved over the Mississippi River to the West in search of land, they traveled across the Great Plains. This huge expanse of grasslands covered over a million square miles. People thought of this area as the Great American Desert. They thought it was incapable of supporting farming. So, they simply crossed the Plains and moved on, with no plans to settle there. Conflict between the settlers heading for Oregon or California and the native peoples of the Plains was rare. Unlike the Hollywood movie scenes, very few wagon trains were attacked. Many Plains Indians helped settlers by selling them supplies and food on the long journey west.

Eventually, farmland in the West became scarce. Immigration to the United States increased rapidly after the Civil War. Then real estate speculators looked to the Great Plains as a source of land for settlers. The resulting conflict over the Plains is often considered the final chapter in the story of cultures in convergence. It is the last place where Native Americans made a stand to preserve their land and independence.

Indian Culture Before the Arrival of the Europeans

As we have seen in studying other areas of North America, Indian tribes were mobile. They moved in response to climatic changes, pressure from other tribes, or the desire for a new and better food source. Nowhere was this more evident than on the Great Plains. Before the thirteenth century C.E., the Plains were sparsely populated by nomadic hunters. In the thirteenth century, the first great population movement into the Plains began. The influx lasted for 600 years. Tribes from the old Mississippian sites moved westward, possibly due to overpopulation. The Pawnee moved from a drought-parched area of what is today northwest Texas to the Platte River area of Nebraska. The

(continued)

The Plains Indians:
Cultures in Final Conflict *(continued)*

Pawnee and other migrants were farmers. They planted squash, corn, and beans. They also hunted pronghorn antelope and buffalo, both found in abundance on the prairie.

A group of people known as the Oceti Sakowin moved into the Wisconsin-Minnesota area. There they hunted and harvested wild rice. These people, whom the French later named the Sioux, had an important impact on the northern Plains. The tribe that probably traveled the farthest was the Apache. One group of Apache traveled from Alberta, Canada, to Montana and then south to the Texas Panhandle. Europeans made their first contact with the Plains Indians in that region in 1514. Spanish explorers led by Francisco Vasquez de Coronado came upon an Apache camp. The Spanish were fascinated by these people. They compared the Apache to the **bedouin**, because of their nomadic existence.

Some Plains Indians settled in agricultural communities along the rivers. But most followed the large herds of game that roamed the prairies. They had small, portable tipis made of poles covered with skins. They used dogs to drag their belongings on the tipi poles. The carrying device was later called a *travois* by the French traders. The most important food source for the Indians was the buffalo. Hunting these large animals on foot took stealth and skill. Before the European settlers came, Plains Indians were living at what is called a **subsistence** level. Food was neither consistent nor plentiful, because of the uncertainty and risk of hunting on foot.

Explorers and Settlers Come to the Land

In the seventeenth and eighteenth centuries, Europeans moved into North America from the East. They crowded the native people of the eastern woodlands. So, the eastern tribes filtered into the Plains. European settlers traded firearms for furs with the eastern tribes. The firearms had a dramatic effect on the movement westward. Aggressive tribes like the Iroquois used guns against other tribes, forcing them to relocate westward. Tribes such as the Omaha, Osage, Missouri, and Ponca pushed out onto the prairie.

The second import from Europe that changed how the Plains Indians lived was the horse. With horses, tribes in the Great Basin and the Rocky Mountains, such as the Comanches, moved eastward onto the Plains to hunt.

Coronado had brought horses on his expedition to the Plains. But more than a century passed before Native Americans were able to acquire these "big dogs," as they called them, in any numbers. Spanish officials in the Southwest prohibited the sale of horses or guns to Native Americans. But the Spaniards trained Indians to care for horses. In 1680, the Pueblo people rose up against Spanish rule. Many Spaniards fled, leaving their horses behind. Through trading and raids, horses spread northward, reaching the Sioux tribes of western Minnesota by 1770. The Plains Indians took to the horse very quickly. They became skillful equestrians and horse breeders.

The horse changed the Plains Indians' way of life from subsistence to abundance. The nomadic hunters could now pursue buffalo for miles, quickly and efficiently. A few mounted hunters could kill enough animals to provide meat for an entire band for a week or more. With such a plentiful food supply, the Plains Indians learned new ways to preserve the meat. They used every part of the buffalo—for shelter, clothing, tools, and ritual articles. A horse could pull a larger travois than a dog. So, tipis could

(continued)

Native Americans:
A Thematic Unit on Converging Cultures

The Plains Indians:
Cultures in Final Conflict (continued)

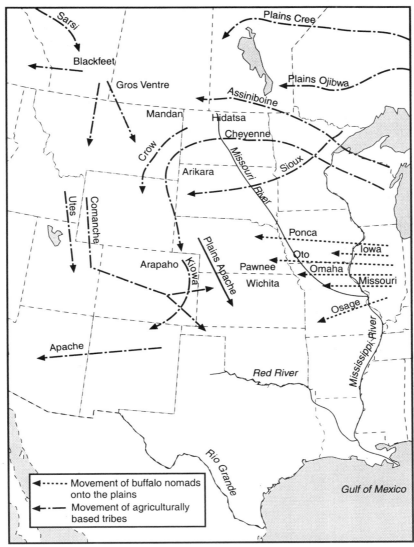

be larger, and the sick and elderly could travel with the band instead of being left behind to die. Horses became a measure of wealth and prestige and a source of intertribal rivalry. This abundant lifestyle, sometimes called the Golden Age of the Plains culture, did not last long. The hunting of buffalo on horseback and the horses' competition for grass started the decline of the buffalo herds. Diseases brought by the nonnative sheep, pigs, and cattle also affected the buffalo population. Most hunting was still done with bow and arrow because guns were too awkward to carry and load while mounted. But traders eventually introduced firearms into the northern Plains.

(continued)

The Plains Indians:
Cultures in Final Conflict (continued)

Rivalries over tribal hunting grounds erupted into warfare. The bloodshed would have been worse except that many Plains tribes had developed a ceremonial warfare called "counting coup." In this ritual, a warrior tried to touch his enemy with a coup stick and then escape without injury. Many tribes considered "counting coup" more challenging and honorable than killing. What did cause an increased death rate was disease brought to the Plains by white traders.

Nomadic tribes were less affected by European diseases than tribes who continued an agricultural way of life. The Mandan and the Hidatsa, who lived in settled communities near trading posts along the western rivers, were devastated by epidemics. Two steamboats sailed up the Missouri River in 1837 to trade for buffalo skins. One crew member had smallpox. The infection spread like wildfire among the native people. Some 10,000 Indians died within a few weeks. The significance of diseases introduced by Europeans in the destruction of native life and culture cannot be overemphasized.

Destruction of the Plains Culture

With the opening of trails to the Far West, settlers and their wagons began crossing the Plains. These early **emigrants** were not interested in the lands of the Plains tribes. But their passage had harmful effects. Settlers' livestock ate the prairie grasses. Settlers killed buffalo or drove them away. Water sources often became polluted. The great trails became dusty, garbage-strewn wastelands. These miles-wide trails cut through migration routes for buffalo herds and Indian tribes. Still, there was little conflict between early settlers and the native people.

The U.S. government, concerned about the ever-increasing westward expansion, sought to guarantee that the Plains Indians would not be a danger in the future. Government officials met at Fort Laramie in 1851 with representatives from several Plains tribes. The two sides negotiated a treaty in which each tribe designated land for its hunting territories and agreed to stay within those boundaries. The treaty ended hundreds of years of Indian migration, following the great herds across the Plains. The government, however, did nothing to preserve the territories created in the treaty. As the century progressed, the government broke treaty after treaty. Encroachment on Indian lands grew in response to pressure from settlers seeking farmland or mining rights.

Worst of all for the Plains Indians was the annihilation of the buffalo, the mainstay of their way of life. Professional hunters armed with high-powered rifles came to the Plains to shoot buffalo. The building of the transcontinental railroad created a demand for meat to feed the construction workers. Then, once the railroad was completed, it was used to transport buffalo hides to the markets back east. In 1871, a new chemical process for tanning leather increased the demand for buffalo hides. Between 1872 and 1874, more than six million buffalo were killed. The buffalo population was estimated at 60 million in 1800. By 1900, it was only a few hundred. The buffalo very nearly became extinct. The government encouraged the hide hunters. Officials saw hunting as a way to make the Indians retire to a **reservation** and adopt white customs and lifestyles. They hoped that, without food, the Indians would become dependent on the government for handouts.

The period following the Civil War was one of warfare between whites and Indians on

(continued)

The Plains Indians:
Cultures in Final Conflict *(continued)*

Railroad passengers shooting at buffalo

the Great Plains. Both sides committed atrocities. In 1864, 700 U.S. troops massacred a peaceful Cheyenne camp at Sand Creek, Colorado. Black Kettle, the Cheyenne chief, flew a white flag of peace along with a U.S. flag that had been given to him by President Lincoln. But the troops, mostly Colorado volunteers, led by Colonel John M. Chivington, killed men, women, and children. In 1866, a group of Sioux warriors under Crazy Horse killed all 80 men in a cavalry unit commanded by Captain William J. Fetterman. And in 1876, the Cheyenne and the Sioux defeated General George Armstrong Custer at the Little Bighorn. Then the government threw all of its military resources against the tribes of the Plains.

In December 1890, one final massacre marked the Plains conflict. Many historians believe that it signaled the end of Indian resistance in the nineteenth century. The 7th U.S. Cavalry was escorting a group of Lakota Sioux to the Pine Ridge Reservation, in South Dakota. At Wounded Knee Creek, a shot was fired. The army responded by killing most of the band. A blizzard prevented burial of the victims for three days. Photographs of the frozen bodies were sold as souvenir postcards. The Massacre at Wounded Knee is the final chapter in the Indian Wars. It is remembered as one of the saddest and most reprehensible events in that struggle.

——— **Glossary of Terms for This Unit** ———

bedouin: A nomadic Arab of the desert areas of North Africa and the Middle East.

emigrants: People who leave one country to enter another. Early settlers to the West were called emigrants because often they were leaving the United States to enter a territory that was not officially part of the United States. Even though places like Oregon and California were eventually added to the United States, the term "emigrant" remained in use.

reservation: A tract of land set aside by the federal government for a specific use, such as providing an area for an Indian people or tribe.

subsistence: The absolute minimum level of food and shelter to sustain existence.

Native Americans:
A Thematic Unit on Converging Cultures

Viewpoints: Whose Land Is It?

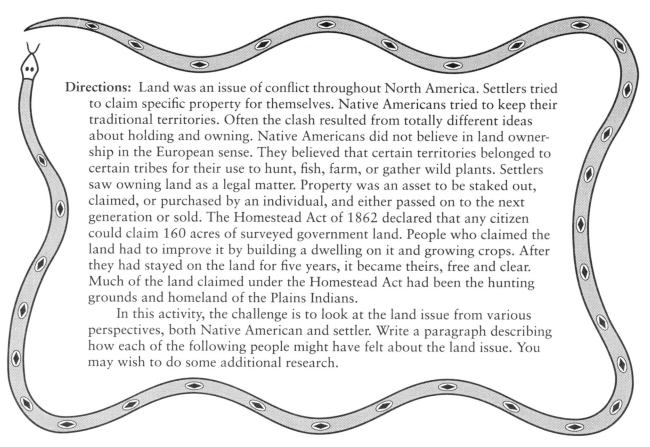

Directions: Land was an issue of conflict throughout North America. Settlers tried to claim specific property for themselves. Native Americans tried to keep their traditional territories. Often the clash resulted from totally different ideas about holding and owning. Native Americans did not believe in land ownership in the European sense. They believed that certain territories belonged to certain tribes for their use to hunt, fish, farm, or gather wild plants. Settlers saw owning land as a legal matter. Property was an asset to be staked out, claimed, or purchased by an individual, and either passed on to the next generation or sold. The Homestead Act of 1862 declared that any citizen could claim 160 acres of surveyed government land. People who claimed the land had to improve it by building a dwelling on it and growing crops. After they had stayed on the land for five years, it became theirs, free and clear. Much of the land claimed under the Homestead Act had been the hunting grounds and homeland of the Plains Indians.

In this activity, the challenge is to look at the land issue from various perspectives, both Native American and settler. Write a paragraph describing how each of the following people might have felt about the land issue. You may wish to do some additional research.

A German immigrant wishing to farm on the Plains
Crazy Horse, leader of the Oglala Sioux
Buffalo Bird Woman of the Hidatsa
A publicity agent for the railroads
Satanta (White Bear), a Kiowa chief
General Philip Sheridan, U.S. Army
A miner hoping to find gold in the Black Hills

Four Great Leaders of the Plains Tribes

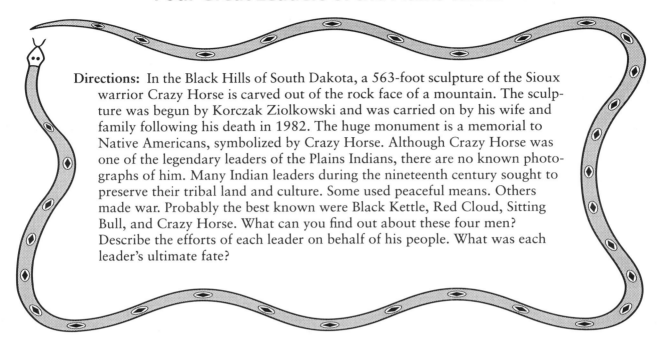

Directions: In the Black Hills of South Dakota, a 563-foot sculpture of the Sioux warrior Crazy Horse is carved out of the rock face of a mountain. The sculpture was begun by Korczak Ziolkowski and was carried on by his wife and family following his death in 1982. The huge monument is a memorial to Native Americans, symbolized by Crazy Horse. Although Crazy Horse was one of the legendary leaders of the Plains Indians, there are no known photographs of him. Many Indian leaders during the nineteenth century sought to preserve their tribal land and culture. Some used peaceful means. Others made war. Probably the best known were Black Kettle, Red Cloud, Sitting Bull, and Crazy Horse. What can you find out about these four men? Describe the efforts of each leader on behalf of his people. What was each leader's ultimate fate?

Black Kettle, Cheyenne chief
Red Cloud, Oglala Lakota (Sioux) chief
Sitting Bull, Hunkpapa Sioux chief
Crazy Horse, Oglala Lakota (Sioux) warrior

Native Americans:
A Thematic Unit on Converging Cultures

A Page from the Past

The Buffalo

The large shaggy beast that has become a symbol of the Plains tribes is not really a buffalo. Unrelated to the Asian water buffalo, it is a uniquely American species known scientifically as *Bison bison*. The American bison received its erroneous name from French trappers. The trappers referred to the animal as *boeuf*, the French word for "beef." At the buffalo's height, there may have been as many as 60 to 75 million on the Plains.

Many of the Plains Indians had always used buffalo meat to supplement the food grown in their settlements. But when the Plains Indians began to hunt on horseback, buffalo became almost the only food that most tribes ate. Buffalo meat was usually consumed at two or three meals a day. Each adult often ate one or two pounds of meat at a meal. Often, the meat was simply roasted. Sometimes it was cooked in a stew with vegetables or cut up and made into a sausage encased in an intestine.

The Plains people preferred fresh meat. But during the winter when hunting was more difficult, they depended on buffalo meat that had been preserved in a number of ways. A long-lasting food called pemmican was made by pounding cooked meat into a paste and mixing it with fat. Sometimes wild berries were added to the mixture. Buffalo meat was also made into jerky by drying it in the sun or smoking it over fires. The jerky lasted for months without spoiling.

No part of the buffalo was wasted. The hide, which often weighed as much as 150 pounds, was particularly valuable. The women were expert in preparing the skin. They stretched out the hide to dry in the sun, fur side down. Then they scraped it to remove bits of flesh and fat. If the hide was to be used for a winter robe, they left the hair on. Otherwise, they soaked the skin in a lye solution, which loosened the hair for removal. Then they made the stiff, hard hide into containers called parfleches. In the parfleches, they stored food, clothing, and other household items.

Women also turned the stiff rawhide into soft leather by using a tanning mixture of fat, brains, liver, and a plant called soaproot. Then they scraped the hide with an elkhorn tool to further soften and stretch it. As many as 20 hides were prepared and sewn together for a large tipi. This product required special skills. So, sometimes women were helped by lodge makers—craftswomen who excelled at designing and assembling tipis. Tanned hides were also used for blankets, shirts, robes, and even diapers.

Buffalo bones were used as parts of sleds or tools. The horns were turned into cups or spoons. Braided rope was made from the long hair at the neck and tail. The sinews became sewing thread. Dried buffalo dung or droppings fueled campfires. A buffalo tail made a handy flyswatter.

The Plains Indians thanked and revered the buffalo for all its bounty. When white hunters found a valuable market for buffalo hides, they hunted the animals nearly to extinction. Usually they left the skinned carcasses to rot on the prairie. Hunting for pleasure or sport also depleted the herds. Such hunting was alien to the Native Americans. They could not understand the waste and destruction of anything natural.

Thanks to conservation, the buffalo is making a comeback. Buffalo is raised commercially for its meat, which is low in cholesterol and fat. Some Indian tribes have their own herds. They use the buffalo for ceremonial hunts to commemorate a vanished way of life, when the buffalo was the lifeblood of the Plains tribes.

A Page from the Past

Chief Joseph

Probably no other nineteenth-century Native American chief has been quoted more often than Chief Joseph. Sometimes referred to as the Indian Napoleon, Joseph was really a pacifist. He abhorred fighting. He did everything in his power to achieve justice for his people, the Nez Percé. He met many times with government officials. Always, he impressed them with his eloquence and intelligence.

The Nez Percé had a long history of good relations with early white settlers. Numbering about 3,600 people, the Nez Percé were horse breeders. They occupied lands in northern Idaho and parts of Washington and Oregon. In 1855, one of the chiefs, Old Joseph, and other Nez Percé leaders signed a treaty with the U.S. government. The treaty ceded a small portion of tribal lands to the government. In 1862, yielding to pressure to open more of the Indian lands for settlement, the government reduced the tribal lands to one tenth their original size. Some Indians signed the new treaty. Old Joseph refused. In 1871, Old Joseph lay dying. He spoke to his son, Young Joseph. "Never forget my dying words. This country holds your father's body. Never sell the bones of your father and mother."

Young Joseph honored his father's words. He argued against ceding any more land to the government. In 1877, Joseph and other leaders were given an ultimatum, or final proposal, by General Oliver Otis Howard. They had to move within 30 days or face the force of the U.S. Army. Joseph reluctantly led his people toward the reservation. As they were preparing to leave, three young

Chief Joseph

Nez Percé men killed four whites. Fearing retaliation, the Nez Percé chiefs led their people toward Canada. There they planned to seek refuge with Sitting Bull.

Over 800 Nez Percé undertook the four-month 1,000-mile journey. They crossed Oregon, Washington, Idaho, and Montana. They came within 40 miles of the Canadian border. Joseph was the best-known leader. So, the conflict between the Nez Percé and the pursuing U.S. troops became known as Chief Joseph's War. The handicaps the Indians faced were formidable. Women and children outnumbered men three to one. Raiding parties of warriors from other tribes stole the Appaloosa horses, for which the Nez Percé were famous. Throughout the trip, the Nez Percé committed no atrocities. They paid farmers and merchants for all supplies and food they obtained along the way. Several times the tribe defeated much larger army forces sent to intercept them. This embarrassed military officials and made them determined to stop the Nez Percé.

Finally, only a short distance from Canada, Colonel Nelson A. Miles and his men surrounded the tribe and attacked. Many of the Indian leaders were killed. Chief Joseph finally gave in, worried about the elderly, wounded, and children. His words of surrender are a testament to his concern for his people. "It is cold, and we have no blankets. The little children are freezing. I am tired. My heart is sick and sad. From where the sun now stands, I will fight no more forever."

Miles had promised that the Nez Percé who surrendered would be allowed to go to the Idaho reservation. Instead, he sent them to Kansas and Oklahoma. There, many died. Chief Joseph's band was kept apart from the rest and eventually sent to a reservation in Washington state. Joseph continued to argue for Indian rights, "The earth is the mother of all people, and all people should have equal rights upon it." When Chief Joseph died, in 1904, the doctor listed the cause of death as a broken heart.

10. American Indians in the Twentieth Century

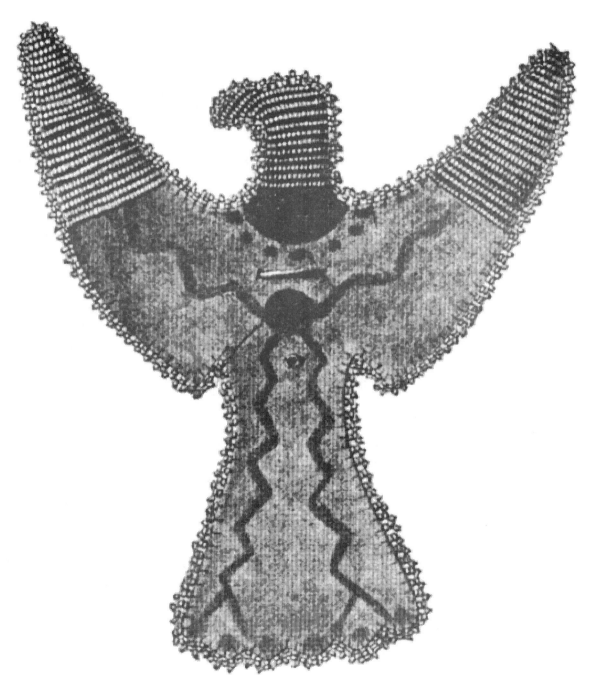

Thunderbird made of rawhide, with bead decorations

American Indians in the Twentieth Century: The Movement Toward Reconciliation and Understanding

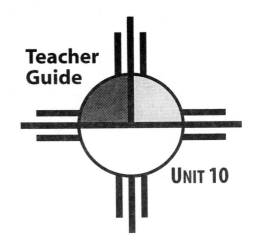

The end of the nineteenth century saw conditions for most Native Americans at their lowest ebb. Many had been forced to reservations that were not part of their traditional lands. Most reservations were cast-off lands which white settlers did not want—barren, isolated, and unproductive. Many tribes lived on government rations. The rations maintained them at subsistence level but made them depend on the government for survival. Some non-Indian Americans were concerned with the plight of Native Americans. But they did not understand how to help. Some well-meaning groups believed that total assimilation into white culture through education, often at boarding schools in the East, was the best way to improve Indians' standard of living. There was little effort to preserve Native American culture. Only stereotypical Indians appeared in advertising or entertainment.

mind about their tribal identity, their cultural background, and how they wish to be governed. Frequently in the twentieth century, Native Americans have had to choose, to decide what traditions, customs, and beliefs they wish to maintain.

This final unit lends itself to a discussion of cultural diversity. Can the United States be a cohesive nation that still recognizes and respects cultural differences? What happens when there is a clash between a cultural standard and the law? A good illustration for this is Quanah Parker, a Comanche leader who was respected by whites and Indians alike. Parker lost a judgeship because he had four wives, a custom acceptable in his culture, but a violation of U.S. law. Your students may be able to think of other examples where individual beliefs based on a particular culture conflict with laws governing the larger population.

Preparation for This Unit

This unit examines how attitudes about Native American culture changed during the twentieth century. It also looks at how difficult it is to find workable solutions for Native American problems in areas such as education, job training, health, and housing. The dilemma is one that faces many groups in America today: how to reconcile cultural diversity with national identity. Not all Native Americans are of one

Student Activities

Activities for this unit can be used as culminating projects for the study of Native Americans. The first asks students to compare the Native American groups they have encountered in the previous units. What cultural similarities can they note? what differences? One of the federal government's most serious and most frequent mistakes in dealing with Native Americans has been not recognizing their great cultural diversity. White officials believed that all Native American groups behaved the same and had the same way of life, attitudes, and culture. Government programs rarely allowed for individual differences among tribes.

The second activity brings the study of Native American groups home to your own area. Students are asked to research a local Native American tribe. Is this tribe autonomous? How are they keeping their unique identity alive? Were there tribes in your locale that are now extinct? A good follow-up project might be to visit museums in your area that have Native American collections or to attend a powwow, if there is one in your area.

American Indians in the Twentieth Century:
The Movement Toward Reconciliation and Understanding

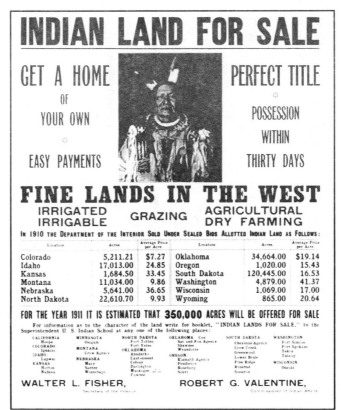

Indian land sale poster

In the 30 years following the Massacre at Wounded Knee, Native Americans found themselves at the worst point in their long history. they were cheated out of tribal lands. They were often forcibly assimilated into white culture. They were not even granted citizenship. They were forgotten people in their own country.

The Dawes Act of 1887 sought to divide up tribal lands and give each Indian family their own parcel. This new practice was called allotment. Each family was to get 160 acres. The idea was to turn Native Americans into individual **entrepreneurs.** The government thought it would break the tribal ties and the reservation system, which encouraged tribal unity. Land

that was left over was sold to whites for farming or mining. Over two million acres in what is now the state of Oklahoma was opened in a great land rush. At noon on a hot day in August 1889, a bugle sounded. Some 50,000 settlers stampeded to stake out land previously designated as permanent Indian territory. They became known as Sooners, because they entered before officially permitted to do so.

Many Native American children were sent east to boarding schools, such as the Carlisle Indian School in Pennsylvania. At these schools, children were forbidden to speak their native language. They had to cut their hair and wear uniforms. They were not allowed to return to

(continued)

American Indians in the Twentieth Century:
The Movement Toward Reconciliation and Understanding
(continued)

their reservations to visit. The idea was to isolate them from their former lives and force them to lose all **vestiges** of their culture. One exception was the Hampton Institute of Virginia. Founded to educate former slaves, Hampton allowed Indian children retain their heritage while learning academic and practical skills. The school museum displayed artifacts from many different cultures to encourage appreciation for diversity. Unfortunately, Hampton's methods were considered controversial. Black and Native American students were allowed to mingle socially, although they were otherwise segregated. The government withdrew Hampton's funding for the education of Native Americans in 1912. The school was forced to rely on private donations.

The turning point for Native Americans finally came during the 1920's. Some 12,000 Native Americans served in the military during World War I in 1917 and 1918. At that time, some Indians could not vote because they had not been granted citizenship. In 1924, Congress passed the Indian Citizenship Act. Individual states, however, often blocked Indians from voting. Arizona, Maine, and New Mexico denied the right to vote to Native Americans until the 1950's. Some tribes ignored citizenship because they considered themselves sovereign nations. To show its independence, the Iroquois Confederacy even issued a separate declaration of war against Germany in World War I.

In the 1920's, small groups of white writers and artists left urban areas to seek **solace** and inspiration in rural settings. The Pueblo country of New Mexico was home to an artist colony. The group became enchanted with Native American art, spiritual beliefs, and atti-

tudes toward nature. They publicized the rich cultural contributions that Native Americans offered to American life.

About the same time, the Indian Rights Association and other organizations began to publicize the government's handling of Indian matters. The Red Progressives were well-educated Indians, dedicated to helping their people. They pushed for a reexamination of government policies. In 1928, the Meriam report was published. This was a study done by the Institute for Government Research and commissioned by the Department of the Interior. It detailed the Native Americans' situation: poor schools, high mortality rate, inadequate housing and health care, and an income level far below that of the rest of the population. The study blamed the government's practice of allotment and the Bureau of Indian Affairs.

Change did not come about immediately. But in 1933, President Franklin D. Roosevelt named reformer John Collier to head the Bureau of Indian Affairs. Collier condemned the policy of allotment. He mandated that Indian cultural and religious beliefs be respected and tolerated. Native American children at government boarding schools no longer had to attend Christian worship services. And once again, Indians were allowed to practice traditional rites, which had been outlawed on reservations.

In 1934, Congress passed the Indian Reorganization Act. This act authorized tribes to organize their own government. They could form corporations to borrow federal money and engage in business enterprises. Unsold surplus lands from allotment reverted to the tribes.

(continued)

American Indians in the Twentieth Century:
The Movement Toward Reconciliation and Understanding
(continued)

Tribes had two years to consider the act before they voted to accept or reject it.

Not all tribes accepted the act. Some who had integrated into white society did not wish to return to a reservation system based on tribal **autonomy**. Not all tribes were cohesive units capable of setting up a complex system of self-government. As was true with other government reforms, the act viewed Native Americans as a single culture rather than unique diverse peoples with different ways of living. Decisions were made for the Indians without consulting them. Nonetheless, the so-called Indian New Deal of the 1930's diminished some of their problems. They were able to make some progress.

Many Native Americans served in World War II. Often they distinguished themselves in battle. Native people also moved to urban areas to work in wartime industries. Their military service and participation in the war effort drew them off the reservations and into mainstream society. Many became aware of how poor living conditions were for their people compared with those of the population as a whole.

After the war, the federal government tried to integrate Native Americans into the larger society. The government also sought less involvement in Indian affairs. One approach was "relocation." Indians were moved from the reservation to urban areas. They were given a bus ticket, an apartment, and an alarm clock to make sure they would be on time for work. They received some job training. But generally they were left to cope on their own.

A second approach was "termination." Under this policy, tribes lost all federal benefits and any treaty rights. They were absorbed into the states where their reservations were located.

Termination proved to be a disaster. Tribes were forced to accept it with little knowledge of what it meant. The Menominee tribe of northeastern Wisconsin had 234,000 acres of timber-rich land. When they were "terminated" in 1954, the tribe had to set up a new Wisconsin county with educational and medical services, and utilities. They also came under new restrictions on how they could raise money and control capital investments. Termination was supposed to free them from all governmental restrictions. Instead, it forced them to sell much of their land. Tribe members fell into poverty.

Policies like termination spurred Native Americans into action. The American Indian Movement (AIM), and other organizations inspired by the civil rights movement of the 1960's, sought to empower Native Americans. In 1969, hundreds of Indians from many different tribes occupied Alcatraz Island in San Francisco Bay. They used the event to publicize the plight of Native Americans. Alcatraz became a symbol of Native American pride. "Red power" became a battle cry during the 1970's. At last, Native Americans spoke out against hundreds of years of exploitation.

Native Americans still face problems. In many cases, reservations remain places of poverty, disease, alcoholism, and drug use. On the other hand, many tribes are taking charge of their destiny. Some tribes have sued successfully to regain ancestral lands. The Passamaquoddy and Penobscot tribes of Maine received $40.3 million dollars to settle their claim to 12 million acres of land. The tribes used the money to purchase 300,000 acres of land and to invest in business enterprises. The Passamaquoddy were particularly successful. They purchased one of

(continued)

American Indians in the Twentieth Century:
The Movement Toward Reconciliation and Understanding
(continued)

the largest blueberry farms in Maine, two radio stations, and the only plant in New England that produces cement.

Several tribes have used a more controversial enterprise to gain money. They have bypassed state regulations prohibiting gambling because reservation land is held under a federal trust. They have set up bingo and other games of chance for the tribe's profit. In Connecticut, the Mashantucket Pequots and the Mohegans have built huge casinos that provide employment and income for the tribes. Some state governments have tried to limit Indian gaming ventures. Businesses in Las Vegas and Atlantic City also oppose them because they compete with casinos and resorts.

Perhaps the most positive thing for Native Americans today is general recognition that Indian culture is an integral part of America, past and present. The Native American is now portrayed in the media as a real person, not as an **anachronism**. A good example is the movie *Dances with Wolves*. In many parts of the country, tribes hold powwows—celebrations of Indian dance, art, and oral tradition. Powwows often draw large crowds of non-Indians who not only are entertained but also learn about Indian culture. Some tribes have educational outreach programs and websites. In Washing-

ton, D.C., the Smithsonian has a new National Museum of the American Indian. Native Americans have been involved in designing the museum, in planning displays, and in administration.

Throughout its history, Native American culture has never been static and unchanging. Indians have adapted to their environment, to technology, and to educational opportunities. The challenge for Native Americans, as for everyone, is to adapt to a changing world and withstand pressures to conform. In that way, all can celebrate the diversity that makes us unique and enriches our national culture.

——— **Glossary of Terms for This Unit** ———

anachronism: Something out of its proper time, usually something that belongs to the past.

autonomy: Independence from the laws of a state or another government; state of being self-governing.

entrepreneurs: People who organize and operate a business venture and assume any risks associated with the venture.

solace: A source of relief.

vestiges: Traces left by something lost.

Name _____

Date _____

UNIT 10   WORKSHEET 1
American Indians in the Twentieth Century:
The Movement Toward Reconciliation and
Understanding

The Disappearance of Indian Lands

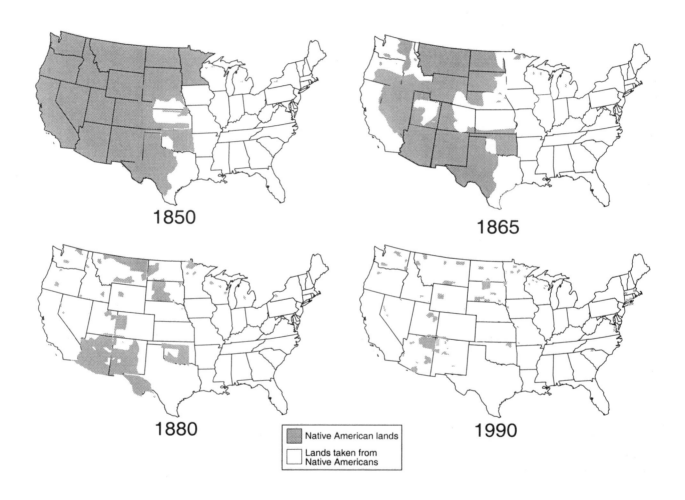

1850

1865

1880

1990

Native American lands

Lands taken from
Native Americans

© 1997 J. Weston Walch, Publisher

Native Americans:
A Thematic Unit on Converging Cultures

Name _____

Date _____

UNIT 10   WORKSHEET 1
American Indians in the Twentieth Century:
The Movement Toward Reconciliation and
Undertanding ˙

Similar or Unique?

Directions: In this study of Native American culture groups, you have looked at many tribes in many different geographic settings. Some cultural traits are shared by most tribes. Other traits are unique to a particular group. Complete the following chart to use for comparing Indian groups. What similarities and what differences do you find?

Culture Group	Geographic Setting	Food Acquisition	Shelter	Clothing	Organization
Mississippian					
Southwest (Pueblo)					
Northern Woodland (Hurons)					
Northeast					
Five Civilized Tribes (Cherokee)					
Pacific Northwest					
California					
Plains					

Name _____

Date _____

UNIT 10   **WORKSHEET 2**
American Indians in the Twentieth Century:
The Movement Toward Reconciliation and
Understanding

Native Americans in Your Community

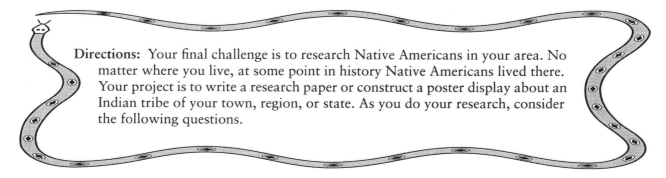

Directions: Your final challenge is to research Native Americans in your area. No matter where you live, at some point in history Native Americans lived there. Your project is to write a research paper or construct a poster display about an Indian tribe of your town, region, or state. As you do your research, consider the following questions.

What larger culture did (does) this tribe belong to?

Does this tribe still exist, or is it extinct like the Yahi of California?

How did this tribe live before Europeans arrived?

Did the tribe consider this their traditional homeland, or did they move here from somewhere else? Were they forced to move by the government?

How did the arrival of European explorers and settlers affect the tribe?

Is the tribe federally recognized by the Bureau of Indian Affairs?

Is there a reservation or territory currently set aside for the tribe?

Is the tribe organized politically with a chief or spokesperson?

Does the tribe participate in any public outreach activities—museums, powwows, educational programs, websites?

Does the tribe own any businesses or other commercial ventures?

How is the tribe (if it still exists) keeping its unique culture—for example, language, traditional crafts, or dance—alive?

Name _____

Date _____

A Page from the Past

Alice Fletcher, the Measuring Woman*

She was known as Her Majesty because she resembled Queen Victoria. In her dress and proper manner, Alice Fletcher appeared every inch a proper Victorian lady. But in her professional work, she went far beyond what most women of her day were able to do. Fletcher was a specialist in Indian culture. She was one of the foremost American anthropologists of the nineteenth century, at a time when most women remained in the home.

Fletcher was born in 1838 in Cuba. Her family had gone to Cuba in hope of improving their father's health. Thomas Fletcher's health did not improve. He died the following year in New York City, where the family had moved. Fletcher was fortunate because her mother was concerned about female education and enrolled her at the age of eight in a pioneering educational institution, the Brooklyn Female Academy. Upon graduation, Fletcher took a job as a governess to escape an abusive stepfather. She left this teaching position in 1870. With financial support from her former employer, she had leisure time to pursue her interest in history and science.

Fletcher was a founding member and an officer of the Association for the Advancement of Women. In the AAW, she found herself in the company of some of the most influential and gifted women of the time. In 1877, the death of her benefactor and a depressed economy left Fletcher without any money. She decided to support herself by giving public lectures, primarily on historical topics. As she traveled the country, she found a growing curiosity about "ancient America" and archaeology. The curator of Harvard University's Peabody Museum of American Archaeology and Ethnology, in Cambridge, Massachusetts, learned of Fletcher's interest and encouraged her to study at the museum.

Fletcher's life changed dramatically in 1881, when she was invited to visit an Omaha Indian reservation in Nebraska. Fletcher was fascinated by the Indians she met. They, in turn, were impressed by her interest in their culture. She met the Sioux chief Sitting Bull. After talking with him, she was convinced that Native Americans had to adopt the white culture if they were to survive. The irony is that she carefully recorded Indian culture to preserve it, but what she advocated was bound to destroy it.

The Office of Indian Affairs hired Fletcher in 1883 to direct the land allotment program for the Omahas. Many people, Fletcher included, felt that individual ownership of land by Indian families, rather than by the tribe, was the key to civilization. Throughout her years of studying various Indian cultures, Fletcher surveyed land and did census counts to allot land to individuals. To the Indians she became known as "the measuring woman."

A lifetime fellowship granted to Fletcher by Mary Thaw, a wealthy Pittsburgh widow, allowed her to study and document tribal customs, dances, ceremonies, and music. She trained a young Omaha, Francis La Flesche, in anthropology. La Flesche became invaluable as a translator and friend. Eventually, Fletcher adopted La Flesche as her son.

Fletcher continued to work throughout her life for the assimilation of Native Americans into white culture. At the same time, she retained a respect for Native American views. In her own words, "Living with my Indian friends, I found I was a stranger in my native land. As time went on, the outward aspect of nature remained the same, but a change was wrought in me. I learned to hear the echoes of a time when every living thing, even the sky, had a voice. That voice, devoutly heard by the ancient people of America, I desire to make audible to others."

---

* Alice Fletcher, *Indian Games and Dances*, v–vi, in Joan Mark, *A Stranger in Her Native Land* (Lincoln, NE: University of Nebraska Press, 1988), p. 354.

Answer Key

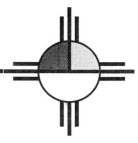

Unit 1: Adena–Hopewell–Mississippian Cultures

Worksheet 1—Comparing Cultures: Cahokia and Ancient Egypt

	Ancient Egypt	Cahokia
Dates for height of culture	c. 2800–1600 B.C.E.	c. 1100 C.E.
Geographic features	Dependent upon Nile River; fertile land near floodplain; good resources—stone and minerals, waterfowl, fish.	Located near floodplain of the Mississippi; fertile land for farming; good resources.
Governmental organization	Absolute rule by a god-king known as a pharaoh.	Ruled by a high chief who also had religious functions.
Social structure	Elite class of priests, relatives of pharaoh, and bureaucrats. Most people were commoners who farmed land.	Elite class of chiefs and religious leaders. Most people were farmers, artisans, traders, or hunters.
Public buildings	Used stone. Religious temples and pyramids built for burials.	Used mounds of earth. Earthworks pyramids for ceremonies and burials.
Writing system	Used hieroglyphics chiseled in stone or written on papyrus.	No written language.
Funerary customs	Bodies of dead were embalmed by mummification. Believed in an afterlife where you brought goods with you from present life.	Dead buried in mounds with possessions. Followers often were sacrificed and buried with the deceased.
Craftsmanship	Used metal for weapons and jewelry. Elaborate stone carving, sculpture, pottery, painting on tomb walls, linen weaving.	Used copper for jewelry and ornaments. Clay pottery. No evidence of painting or cloth making.
Ways of making a living (farming? trade?)	Farming most important; trade and craftsmanship also significant.	Farming and hunting most important; trade and making crafts for trade also significant.
Religious beliefs	Polytheistic; gods control nature; strong belief in the afterlife as evidenced by elaborate burials.	Belief in nature gods, spirits; belief in afterlife; elaborate burials for chiefs and priests. Sun may have been important supernatural force.
Role of women	Women active in Egyptian society; they could own property and engage in business. One pharaoh was a woman, Queen Hatshepsut.	Women's role unclear. In one burial, over 25 young women were sacrificed. An honor or a punishment?

Unit 2: Arctic Amerindians

Worksheet 1—Who Really "Discovered" America?

Explorer	Date	Landfall	Type of Seagoing Craft	Historical Evidence	Probability of Discovery (my opinion)
Saint Brendan	sixth century C.E.	unknown	curragh	Story of voyage written in eighth-century book.	Voyage re-created in 1977.
Madog (Madoc) Gwynedd of Wales	1170 C.E.	Mobile Bay, Alabama	wooden ship	Oral and written stories; many reports of "Welsh-speaking" Indians.	
The Chinese (Hui-Shen)	fifth century C.E.	Mexico or California	junk	Seventh-century Chinese records; Chinese anchor stones found in Los Angeles harbor.	
The Egyptians	2000 B.C.E.– first century C.E.	Central America	reed boat	Cultural similarities between Amerindians and Egyptians.	Trip re-created by Thor Heyerdahl.
The Phoenicians	first century B.C.E.	East Coast	open boat	Dighton Rock in Massachusetts purported to have Phoenician script on it.	
Leif Eriksson	1000 C.E.	Newfoundland	long boat	Viking artifacts found at L'Anse aux Meadows, in Newfoundland.	
(Bonus) Henry Sinclair of Scotland	1394 C.E.	East Coast	unknown	Written story about the trip. A rock in Westford, Massachusetts, supposedly has crest of Gunn Clan carved into it.	
Others					

Unit 2: Arctic Amerindians

Worksheet 2—Cultures in Convergence

1. Wampanoag   England   (Massachusetts area)
2. Cherokee   Spain and England   (Southeast—Georgia, Carolinas)
3. Pueblo   Spain   (Southwest)
4. Huron   France   (Great Lakes area, north of Lake Ontario)
5. Lakota   France   (Originally Minnesota area, later moved to Great Plains)
6. Tlingit   Russia   (Alaska)
7. Calusa   Spain   (Florida)
8. Yani   Spain   (California)
9. Powhatan   England   (Virginia)
10. Fox   France   (Michigan)

Unit 4: Indian Cultures of the Great Lakes Legion

Worksheet 2—Cultural Exchanges

Religious Beliefs

Native Americans did convert to the Roman Catholicism of the French, but the French really did not participate in the traditional native spiritual beliefs. A few French traders and trappers who took Indian wives might join in tribal ceremonies and religious rituals.

Food

Although trappers and traders in the "wild" might depend upon such Indian foods as game, wild plants, and indigenous cultivated crops, most preferred imported European foodstuffs. Native Americans developed a taste for flour and sugar, and these became popular trade items.

Clothing

Native Americans liked the bright-colored cloth that European traders offered, and as time went on they used this material for clothes. French traders and trappers often adopted the buckskin clothing of Native Americans because of its durability.

Transportation

The French borrowed the native canoe for water transportation and found it much superior to their skiffs. Trappers, traders, and colonists also adopted Indian snowshoes.

Housing

Some Indians eventually had timber or stone houses like those built by European settlers, but most retained their longhouses. Europeans did not adopt any Native American housing styles.

Unit 7: The Five Civilized Tribes and the New American Nation

Worksheet 2—The Trail Where We Cried: The Removal of Native Americans from the Southeast

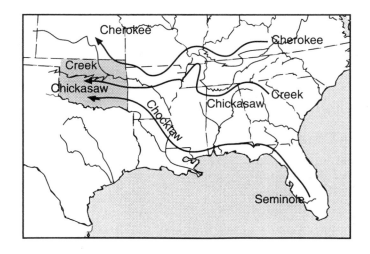

Unit 9: The Plains Indians

Worksheet 2—Four Great Leaders of the Plains Tribes

Black Kettle, one of the Cheyenne chiefs, was aware of the strength of the U.S. military and hoped to protect his people by avoiding war at all cost. Black Kettle even agreed to breaking the Fort Laramie Treaty of 1851, which had assigned land to the Plains tribes. Black Kettle and White Antelope, another Cheyenne leader, traveled to Washington, D.C., to meet with President Lincoln, who gave the chiefs a large American flag and a peace medal. Frightened by rumors of an Indian War, Black Kettle traveled to Denver to meet with the territorial governor of Colorado and the military commander of the area, Colonel John Chivington. Black Kettle pleaded that all he wanted was peace for his people and was told he would be safe camping near Fort Lyon. Black Kettle and his band camped at Sand Creek, near the fort. On November 29, 1864, Chivington and his troops attacked the Indians as they slept. White Antelope was killed, along with 150 other Cheyenne. The army even scalped and mutilated the bodies of their victims and destroyed the village and its supplies. Black Kettle miraculously escaped, along with a few other survivors, and sought aid from another group of Cheyenne. Despite being deceived, he did not go to war. In 1868, Black Kettle settled his people along the Washita River on a reservation. That November, George Armstrong Custer led his troops into Black Kettle's village and killed Black Kettle, his wife, and over 100 other Cheyennes. Although some Cheyenne had resisted against the U.S. government, Black Kettle had not, and he never lost hope that he and his people would be allowed to live in peace.

Red Cloud was born on the Platte River, in Nebraska Territory, in 1822. By the 1860's, the Oglala Sioux recognized him as one of their leaders. Red Cloud and his warriors successfully forced the United States to shut down traffic on the Bozeman Trail, which led across Sioux territory to the mines of Montana. The government had not mentioned that it planned to construct a series of forts and increase military presence. Red Cloud forced the government to abandon the forts in 1868. He signed a peace treaty at Fort Laramie in 1868, which declared that the Indians would no longer make war and would settle on a large reservation north of Nebraska in return for money and other gifts. Most Native Americans who signed the treaty did not truly understand its wording, which was very complex. The Indians soon found out that they had been deceived—they had agreed to move into territory that was not land they considered their homeland, and the government gifts were of poor quality. Red Cloud did not go to war again, but he traveled to Washington four times to meet with the president. He gave speeches to groups in the East who sympathized with Indian claims of poor treatment. His forceful arguments won him an agency (designated territory) for his own people near the North Platte River, which is where he wanted it. Meanwhile, other Sioux lost trust in Red Cloud because they felt that he had sold out to the whites in return for gifts. Red Cloud himself stated that he would not go to war with the whites ever again, that others must carry on the war. The government eventually moved Red Cloud's people farther north, going back on their earlier promise. Red Cloud lived out the remainder of his days attempting to exist peacefully with whites while continually fighting for Indian rights and protesting mistreatment of Indians. He did not fight at Little Bighorn, but encouraged those who did. Red Cloud died in 1909, at the age of 87. He remains a controversial figure among Indians and whites alike.

Sitting Bull, the great war chief of the Lakota Sioux, had not accepted the Treaty of Fort Laramie that created a Sioux reservation north of the Missouri River in the Dakotas. Matters came to a head when the army decided to build a fort in the Black Hills to guard the Northern Pacific Railroad. Custer led an expedition to find a good location for the fort and discovered gold. With thousands of prospectors and other settlers rushing into the Black Hills, the army decided that Sitting Bull and his people had to be made to stay on a reservation. In 1876, Sitting Bull led a confederation of Sioux and Cheyenne warriors to decisive victory over Custer at the Little Bighorn River in Montana. After the battle, Sitting Bull and his followers, pursued by the army, fled to Canada. In 1881, Sitting Bull was offered amnesty, and he returned to the United States and settled on the Standing

Rock Reservation, in North Dakota. In 1889 to 1990, a new religion called the Ghost Dance swept across the Indian tribes of the West. Originating with a medicine man named Wokova, the Ghost Dance religion taught that if the Indians danced in a new ritual, the whites would disappear, Indian ancestors would return to life, and buffalo would once more dominate the plains. Government officials, fearful that Sitting Bull was causing unrest among his followers, sent a party of Indian policeman to arrest the chief. A scuffle broke out, and Sitting Bull and seven of his followers were killed. Sitting Bull was probably one of the best known Indian chiefs due to his participation in Buffalo Bill's Wild West Show and his victory at Little Bighorn.

Crazy Horse was best known as an Oglala Lakota warrior-chief. Incidents in his youth convinced Crazy Horse that white people could not be trusted, and he took this belief with him onto the warpath. He led Sioux warriors on the Fetterman massacre, where 80 government soldiers were lured into a trap and killed. His deeds made his people acknowledge him as a war leader when he was only 25. In 1876, Crazy Horse was a leader in both the Battle of the Rosebud and the Battle of Little Bighorn. These Indian victories caused the United States to intensify the military presence and increase the number of campaigns against the Lakota, who had not agreed to stay on a reservation. In 1877, Crazy Horse's band surrendered, one of the last to do so. He brought his people to Fort Robinson, where he believed he could have his own agency. The commander of the fort tried to take Crazy Horse into custody, frightened by rumors that he was plotting against the government. Crazy Horse resisted, and a guard stabbed him with a bayonet. He died that night at the age of 36. Crazy Horse remains a symbol of Indian resistance to the present day.

Bibliography

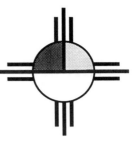

This book list is not designed to be inclusive, but should give teachers a starting point in finding materials for their own personal research as well as classroom use. All of these resources are appropriate for student use. Many of them have been chosen because of their superb maps and illustrations as well as the print material.

Publications of General Interest

Native Peoples Magazine is published by the National Museum of the American Indian, the Smithsonian Institution, and other organizations. *Native Peoples* also has an education program that provides material to students and teachers to help them better understand the "tremendous contributions made to the world by native peoples of the Americas." For subscription services, call 602-252-2236 or write P.O. Box 36820, Phoenix, AZ 85067-6820. For the education program, contact Rush Scott, *Native Peoples Magazine* Education Program, 5333 North Seventh Street, Suite C-224, Phoenix, AZ 85014-2804, 602-252-2236.

The American Indian is the title of an entire series of books on Native Americans published by Time-Life Books beginning in 1992. Books in the series are divided by cultural groups. They are very detailed and include up-to-date research and excellent illustrations. Each volume also has an extensive bibliography. The following list includes books particularly useful in studying individual units in this book.

The First Americans, The American Indian. Alexandria, VA: Time-Life Books, 1992.

People of the Ice and Snow, The American Indian. Alexandria, VA: Time-Life Books, 1994.

The European Challenge, The American Indian. Alexandria, VA: Time-Life Books, 1992.

People of the Desert, The American Indian. Alexandria, VA: Time-Life Books, 1993.

Realm of the Iroquois, The American Indian. Alexandria, VA: Time-Life Books, 1993.

Keepers of the Totem, The American Indian. Alexandria, VA: Time-Life Books, 1993.

The Indians of California, The American Indian. Alexandria, VA: Time-Life Books, 1994.

The Buffalo Hunters, The American Indian. Alexandria, VA: Time-Life Books, 1993.

The Reservations. The American Indian. Alexandria, VA: Time-Life Books, 1995.

Mound Builders and Cliff Dwellers, The American Indian. Alexandria, VA: Time-Life Books, 1992.

Erdoes, Richard, and Alfonse Ortiz, eds. *American Indian Myths and Legends*. New York: Pantheon Books, 1984.

Hoxie, Frederick E., ed. *Encyclopedia of North American Indians*. Boston: Houghton Mifflin Co., 1996.

Josephy, Alvin M., Jr. *500 Nations*. New York: Alfred A. Knopf, 1994. The companion volume to the television documentary of the same title. Contains beautiful illustrations and photographs as well as commentaries by contemporary Native Americans.

Kopper, Philip. *The Smithsonian Book of North American Indians: Before the Coming of the Europeans*. Washington D.C.: Smithsonian Books, 1986.

Milanich, Jerald T., and Susan Milbrath, eds. *First Encounters: Spanish Explorations in the Caribbean and the United States, 1492–1570*. Gainesville: University of Florida Press, 1989.

SIRS, Inc., published a beautiful series of photo-essays on Native Americans. These would be valuable for challenged learners. (SIRS, Inc., P.O. Box 2348, Boca Raton, FL 33427-2348; telephone 1-800-232-SIRS.)

Taylor, Colin F., and William C. Sturtevant. *The Native Americans*. New York: Smithmark Books, 1991. A large coffee-table book, with good scholarly research. Treats Native Americans by culture group and has beautiful collages of native art, dress, and tools.

Thomas, David Hurst, et al. *The Native Americans, An Illustrated History*. Atlanta: Turner Publishing, 1993. Unusual photographs as well as artwork by Native American artists make this book an excellent source. Contributors are also renowned scholars in the field.

Viola, Herman J. *After Columbus: The Smithsonian Chronicle of the North American Indians*. Washington: Smithsonian Books, 1990. Highly recommended. An excellent summary of the contact between the settlers and the North American continent and its native peoples. Unusual photos and artwork.

Viola, Herman J., and Carolyn Margolis. *Seeds of Change*. Washington: Smithsonian Institution Press, 1991. A must for any school library, this book was published for the Columbus Quincentennial and explores the interaction and exchanges between Old and New Worlds.

Ward, Geoffrey C. *The West*. Boston: Little, Brown and Company, 1996. The companion volume to the PBS series. Lavishly illustrated.

Media Resources

There are many videos about Native Americans and more come out literally weekly. Some excellent sources for these videos are given below.

The Jefferson Expansion National Historical Association has a wonderful book and video catalog of American western history that includes Native Americans. The catalog is called Gone West! (11 North Fourth Street, St. Louis, MO 63102; telephone 1-800-537-7962). Proceeds from the sales generate donations to National Park Service programs.

PBS Video has many videos dealing with Native American topics, including *The West* and Ric Burns's *The Way West*.

Zenger Media, a part of Social Studies School Service, is a very inclusive source with an entire section devoted to Native American Studies. Some videos available are the *500 Nations* series and an *American Experience* episode, "Ishi, The Last Yahi." CD-ROMs are also included, among them *The American Indian: A Multimedia Encyclopedia* and *Explorers of the New World*. Zenger Media, 10200 Jefferson Boulevard, Room 94, P.O. Box 802, Culver City, CA 90232-0802; telephone 1-800-421-4246.

One way to access information about Native American groups is through the Internet, particularly the World Wide Web. This information is usually current and up to date, but we need to practice some caution in accessing Internet materials. We teach students to evaluate and be selective about library materials. We also must teach students how to evaluate Web resources and to avoid the abundant cybergarbage. The skill of separating the useful information from the trivial promotes lifelong learning.

In researching the World Wide Web, it is helpful (if not essential) to have some sort of Web browser like Netscape which can connect you easily to the different search engines like Alta Vista, Yahoo, Lycos, and Webcrawler. Using these search services, you can often simply type in the key words like "Native American Art" or "Cherokee Nation" and get some interesting results. Alta Vista gives you a synopsis of the Web sites, while Webcrawler simply lists them by the name of the site. There are hundreds of sites pertaining to Native American culture and history. Here are a few Web sites to give you an idea of what can be accessed:

http://www.info.pitt.edu/~imitten/indian.html
Native American site designed by Lisa Mitten, a mixed blood Mohawk and librarian at the University of Pittsburg. Very extensive with good links to many sites.

http://latino.sscnet.ucla.edu/native.links.html
Contains Listservs, Gophers, and Web sites pertaining to Native American topics.

http://www.maxwell.syr.edu/nativeweb
A site called "Native Web—a cyber-place for the Earth's indigenous peoples." Has bibliographies, newsletters, K-12 educational resources, and much more.

http://www.dickshovel.com/compacts. html
Contains short histories of many tribes with bibliographies. Part of a project that will eventually contain histories of 240 tribes.

http://www.si.edu/nmai/
The National Museum of the American Indian. View exhibits and find out about the museum's resources and the new building being constructed on the mall in Washington, D.C.

http://www.axess.com/mohawk/iroquois/iroquois.html
The Iroquois Confederacy Information Section. This site contains links to Iroquois stories and legends as well as many other historical resources.

http://www.phoenix.net/~martikw/
History of the Cherokee. Maintained by a member of the Oklahoma band of Cherokee, this site has good links to other Native American sites.

About the Authors

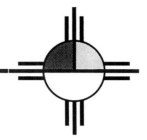

Wendy S. Wilson has been a teacher in the Lexington, Massachusetts, public schools since 1971. She has taught social studies in grades 7 to 12 and is also a senior lecturer in history at University College, Northeastern University. She is a coauthor of other Walch publications, *American History on the Screen* with Gerald H. Herman, and *Ellis Island and Beyond* and *Heading West* with Jack Papadonis. She has done extensive consulting and is a frequent presenter at conferences.

Lloyd M. Thompson was a teacher in the Boston public schools for 22 years. He has taught social studies, reading, and English in grades 7 to 11. Now retired from teaching, he is engaging in extensive research into Native American history, particularly that of his Abenaki ancestors. This is the first time the two authors have collaborated to write a book, although they have been married for 25 years and share an interest in history and archaeology that keeps their bookshelves bulging.

Share Your Bright Ideas with Us!

We want to hear from you! Your valuable comments and suggestions will help us meet your current and future classroom needs.

Your name_____Date_____

School name_____Phone_____

School address_____

Grade level taught_____Subject area(s) taught_____Average class size_____

Where did you purchase this publication?_____

Was your salesperson knowledgeable about this product?   Yes_____   No_____

What monies were used to purchase this product?

____School supplemental budget   ____Federal/state funding   ____Personal

Please "grade" this Walch publication according to the following criteria:

Quality of service you received when purchasing	A	B	C	D	F
Ease of use	A	B	C	D	F
Quality of content	A	B	C	D	F
Page layout	A	B	C	D	F
Organization of material	A	B	C	D	F
Suitability for grade level	A	B	C	D	F
Instructional value	A	B	C	D	F

COMMENTS:_____

_____

What specific supplemental materials would help you meet your current—or future—instructional needs?

_____

Have you used other Walch publications? If so, which ones?_____

May we use your comments in upcoming communications?   ____Yes   ____No

Please **FAX** this completed form to **207-772-3105**, or mail it to:

Product Development, J.Weston Walch, Publisher, P.O. Box 658, Portland, ME 04104-0658

We will send you a **FREE GIFT** as our way of thanking you for your feedback. **THANK YOU!**